...this book should carry a health warning for priests. They might be infected by the author's passionate enthusiasm for priesthood – or intoxicated by the rich cocktail of quotations he has mixed ...

— *Kevin Kelly, moral theologian, Parish Priest and author, Liverpool*

... this book is filled with gentle, poetic encouragement for priests – and others – to find that balance between head and heart which will sustain them in their ministry and allow them to accept the ministry of others ...

— *Therese Vanier (of the L'Arche Communities), London*

... an honest analysis of the pressures and questions in the life and ministry of today's priest. In the course of its reflections it never loses sight of the spirituality, the emotions and struggles of the man of flesh and blood who finds himself called to be priest. Especially his desire to be faithful. It is a loving look at the goodness of priests, trying to serve the beauty in people. The book gives hope.

— *Colm Kilcoyne, Parish Priest and author, Co Mayo*

... an original and exciting attempt to find fresh images and symbols to help priests reconstruct their identity for a new era in the life of the church. It is a passionate plea for priests to develop interiority and personal growth in the context of community. The sacramentality of the whole of the life of the priest is beautifully and poignantly spelt out. The book is full of the pain and poetry of life. All who are involved in initial formation for secular or religious priesthood, or with spiritual direction or renewal programmes, or who are trying to revitalise their own spirit of priesthood could benefit from reading this challenging and timely book.

— *Moya Curran, Director of Pastoral Studies,*
All Hallows College, Dublin

New Hearts for New Models is both fearless and imaginative. Courageous disclosure about where we are, and what we hope for, is a necessary prerequisite for honest conversation about the future of priesthood, the religious life and the priestly people. The freedom to be creative is the gift of the creative God. And imagination must leaven the conversation ...

—   *h Priest and author, Liverpool*

D1501017

As with all the artisans who build holiness, wholeness and beauty within the hearts of others; as with all the artists who enrich our lives through their creativity and imagination; as with all the teachers who reveal within our pain, the face of God, there is a precious art, too, in being a priest of life … If humanity is to be redeemed by compassion, if the world is to be saved by justice-makers, if peace and love are ever to light our days with each morning's sun, then, O Mystery of Life, send us priests of passion … (Daniel Dancing Fish, Sacramento, 1990)

A diocesan priest needs maturity. He needs enough maturity to say to himself: 'No one else is going to construct a spiritual framework for my life. If I don't do it, it won't get done. And without a spiritual framework, priesthood makes no sense.' And the diocesan priest's only community is the presbyterate of his diocese and the people of his parish. We are singularly bereft of safety nets. (Tony Philpot, NCP Paper, Birmingham, 1997)

Never has the interior life of today's priest been so important to his spiritual and personal health, and to his effectiveness as pastor and shepherd, as it is during this time of seeking and waiting … The priest's task is to minister to the faithful. But if he is also one of the faithful (as he truly is) then he has to minister to himself as well. 'Keep watch over yourselves and over all the faithful … (Acts 20:28) … Thomas Merton wrote to the Gethsemani novices, 'Prayer is the response to God within us, the discovery of God within us; it leads ultimately to the discovery and fulfilment of our own true being in God' … But our inner life does not exist in isolation. In God, priest and people are truly one with each other. The priest is one with each and every one of them, and all of them with him. We all meet in God. (Donald Cozzens, The Spirituality of the Diocesan Priest)

Daniel J. O'Leary

New Hearts
for New Models

A SPIRITUALITY FOR PRIESTS TODAY

the columba press

First published in 1997 by
Τhe columBa press
55a Spruce Avenue, Stillorgan Industrial Park,
Blackrock, Co Dublin

Cover by Bill Bolger
Origination by The Columba Press
Printed in Ireland by Colour Books Ltd, Dublin
ISBN 1 85607 219 3

Acknowledgements

The author and publishers gratefully acknowledge the permission of the following to use substantial quotations from works within their copyright: Gracewing Fowler Wright Ltd, Mowbray [Cassell PLC], Orbis Books, Darton, Longman and Todd, Forest of Peace Books Inc., and the editors of *The Furrow*, *The Way* and *The Way Supplement*. Individual quotations are fully credited in the end notes.

Contents

PART THREE
Working from where we are

Preface

This book was written during my sixth year as parish priest at St Benedict's, Garforth, in Yorkshire. Even while we were busy designing, funding, and now building a new church, another sacred place of worship and service was also growing within our hearts. Both the church and the book were fashioned out of that sacred space – the parish's community spirit and its sense of compassionate, collaborative ministry.

These pages are dedicated, therefore, to those whose love, understanding and forgiveness have changed my life by revealing to me some deeper dimensions of priesthood and of my humanity. Without the trust, support and inspiration of so many faith-filled people, especially those women who have been 'soul-friends' to me, my hope, my energy, my belief in God, in the church, and in myself would have burned very low at times. Such people have come into my life like rays of lovely light, telling me that tomorrow is another day, that once down is no battle, that faith is about believing in the dawn while it is still dark.

Among the priests I have known, there are those who have personified for me the true meaning of priesthood. Sensitively and compassionately, they have never con-demned, blamed or ridiculed, only carefully understood – especially my brother, Mícheál, whose wisdom and love I treasure. My Mom and sister Maura, too, are forever an in-spiration, as is my native parish of Rathmore, Co Kerry, where our celtic roots are alive and well in the tradition of Sliabh Luachra. As a beacon of hope, All Hallows College, Dublin, where I was ordained, is now a fine example of vision and strategies, during these threshold years of turnings, in the shaping of ministries for a demanding, dynamic but uncertain future.

Without the support of Margaret Siberry, Mary Nicholas, Sr Monica O'Sullivan, Philip Holdroyd and Jim O'Keefe – advisers, encouragers and proof-readers – I doubt if these pages would ever have seen the light of day.

And finally, my thanks to Seán O Boyle of The Columba Press. May his commitment to the Word – the word of good books, of good news and of good welcomes – forever increase his store.

Introduction

This little book was started on its way by a few ordinary priests, doing their ordinary work, asking a few ordinary questions about their lives. For that reason it is not meant to be a profound piece of research about the theology, scriptural exegesis or history of ordained priesthood, necessary as such a basis may be for what follows. There are, however, as most priests know, many easily-available, excellent and scholarly works on these current concerns of priests, for those who wish to pursue, more closely, such important areas of study.[1]

To be sure, the notes in this book are deeply influenced by the generally-agreed directions offered by the scholarly caretakers of our best traditions. Thus grounded, it tries to avoid all escapist flights-of-fancy about a disconnected priesthood in a hypothetical future. But its aim is modest. Its purpose is simply to acknowledge and reflect upon, in a realistic way, a few of the challenging situations in which we, diocesan priests, find ourselves today, and to offer some comments about a nourishing and personal spirituality that are rooted in the past, acknowledged in the present, and, out of that context, to suggest some possibilities for today and tomorrow. Among the many elements that it tries to hold in balance, a predominant one is that perennial tension between mind and heart.

This tension is not new in Christianity. Sometimes the tension has been expressed in terms of the reasons of the heart that the mind can never know. The letter to the Hebrews describes the word of God as 'living and active, sharper than any two-edged sword, piercing until it divides soul from spirit, joints from marrow; it is able to judge the thoughts and intentions of the heart'. (Heb 4:12.) Only the word of God can penetrate into the innermost and most intimate areas of the heart of the preacher of the word, into the heart of every hearer of the word, into the heart-to-heart relationship between preacher and hearer, and between hearer and hearer.[2]

There are two important points I wish to make, right at the beginning, about the thrust and purpose of this book. In the first place, it is offered only as an introduction to a 'conversation'. There are huge issues about the future of priesthood that are not addressed here. As I write this introduction, for instance, the National Conference of Priests for England and Wales, (Sept 1997) is committing itself to exploring the 'uncharted waters' in which priesthood finds itself, during these years of complex and unprecedented change. There is the rapidly increasing secularistion of our society, the growing autonomy of young people, the silent plea of the victims of injustice and poverty as they try to find their voice in a culture of 'social exclusion'. There is also the reality of a media-centred world, of unbelievable advances in the human sciences, and of a technology that is barely imaginable. All of this, and much more, needs to be carefully considered in any realistic effort to come to terms with the role of priesthood today.

In the second place, I wish to make it clear that the purpose of the book is not to widen the gap between the ordained ministry and the priesthood of all the baptised faithful. There is no intention to attribute to priests only, what is the privilege and duty of every Christian. The models and images outlined in the book are intended to heal a deep-seated dualism that damages the spiritual health of our church, and of the priesthood. The priest is called to be the embodiment, the sacrament, of what every Christian is called to be. In one of his comments to me about the draft of this book, Jim O'Keefe, President of Ushaw College, Durham, wrote, 'I reckon that it is the job of the whole church and everyone in it, to do what you're asking of priests, but that it is the more specific call of the priest to ensure that it is done – it does not matter too much if he is not so good at it all by himself!'

Part One – Gathering the Energy, is an honest look at the way many priests see their lives today, and about fanning alive again that often flickering flame within us, to provide energy for new beginnings. *Part Two – Creating the Models*, is about sketching out some possible shapes and images for our ministry today. These models are intended to deepen, enrich, explore and expand the roles we already try to fill, especially our role in the celebration of the sacraments. In *Part Three – Working from Where We Are*, a brief critique is offered of the negative and positive influences on, and conditions of, our priesthood today, that hinder or help the living out of the suggested models; it also assesses the chances of break-through and development, given the conditions, limitations and possibilities in our ministry.

I have taken the liberty of including some Discussion Points at the end of each Part. Please send me, c/o The Columba Press, any constructive criticism or other reactions that might contribute to future developments in this area of our spirituality and roles.

Like every human being, priests are very earthen vessels carrying an immense treasure. Our fragile hearts may well be filled with apprehension at some of the challenges and expectations placed on us in the following pages. But in the middle of our dark sinfulness and in the muddle of our confusion and struggle, we are held, so passionately, by our tremendous Lover of Light. G.A. Stoddart Kennedy wrote:

> Night shadowed all, and wandering winds came
> wailing from afar,
> But out across the darkening sea shone forth
> one single star.

PART I

Gathering our Energy

The here and now

To begin with, there is a growing sense of isolation, confusion and disillusionment among many priests today. For a variety of reasons including diminishing congregations, shortage of priests, scandals within the ranks, and a growing sense of responsibility among the laity, an ever-increasing number of priests feel that their role is becoming either distorted or diminished, and their unique contribution undervalued.

Is it too much to hope that the new optimism drawing and driving so many Christians forwards during these pre-millennium years, even at a time of widespread antipathy and pessimism, will catch fire in the heart of every priest? What needs to be tackled now is the strange malaise and doubt that springs from a newly-felt loneliness and from a lack of self-esteem and self-identity in our lives as priests during this critical transition time for the church. While trying to avoid the 'alarmist' tag on the one hand, and the 'head-in-the-sand' syndrome on the other, it is fairly clear to anyone who listens and talks to priests at clergy conferences and other meetings of priests and laity, that attitudes ranging somewhere between desperation and resignation are daily and honestly expressed. Now is the time, therefore, not for a dismantling or reconstruction of the priesthood arising from the compulsions of our time, but for a creative revisioning of its essential nature, aimed at restoring the joy of being a priest today in a world in sore need of spiritual values.

In his book *A Priesthood in Tune*, Thomas Lane suggests that with the inroad of many new forms of secularism, it would seem that we are involved in a call for a kind of Copernican revolution in the lifestyle, work, and prayer-style of those in ordained ministry (p. 207). And Joan Chittister, surely a prophet for our times, in her *The Fire in these Ashes*, gathers up the wisdom of her decades of experience in working with sisters and priests all over the world. It is an excellent little book. She writes about the here and now. She not only warns about the temptation to retreat into the recesses of a past security, but also fabricating romantic dreams of a possible, but unreal future. The real question is concerned with what constitutes an authentic spirituality for religious and diocesan priests today.

She points out that everyday, thoughtful religious (and diocesan priests) face or wrestle with the really current questions in their lives: Am I wasting my life in this kind of work? Should I encourage others to join us? What is the spiritual substance of my priestly life? Is the current style of priesthood dying, or rising, or both? The truth of the answer is obvious and painful, apparent and exciting at the same time: There is only one place that is holy and that place is the here and now. The fire in the ashes, the burning sanctity to be blown into flame, is not in the past or future, but in the space that is in-between the respected old and the emerging new, the one that is pioneering, the one that is in process in a world reeling from the permanency of change at a step-over moment in history.[1]

This revisioning calls for much openness and deep soul-searching for each priest. The whole thrust of this book is fired by the conviction that the greening of the priesthood can only begin if we, as priests, are prepared to make the long, difficult journey into our own humanity. This is a particularly precarious journey for many priests to make. At least for those of us in the second half of life, almost

everything in our training, in the expectations of parishioners about our role, in a world of clericalism and institutionalism, combines to make us doubtful, resistant, and
cynical about undertaking such an adventure. (This very
statement, for instance, will be rejected by many priests as
untrue, and rightly so, if their experiences of ministry and
celibacy have brought them to the place where they truly
wish to be.)

The models of priesthood presented in these pages are developed from the way Jesus formed his communities and,
before that, on the way that God began to win the hearts of
humanity – by the spreading of the Good News from one
small baby, all over the world. As each individual heart
picks up that first call to conversion and conviction from
another, like fire catches and spreads in the dry stubble of
a summer field, so too does God's intense desire for community draw and drive us into the family of human and
divine loving.

There is a perennial debate about priorities when it comes
to structuring models for priesthood. Should the emphasis
be on the 'inner work' or the 'outer work', on 'the active
life' or the 'contemplative one', on the 'Martha model' or
'the Mary one'? But it is clear enough, without getting lost
in the semantics of the debate, that both models need each
other. For some priests, the life of prayer is the means of
discovering the face of God: for others, God's face is discovered in the faces of the poor. For both, however, *some*
kind of contemplation is the beginning and the end of the
enterprise. We must first have the vision, and then we
must 'work the vision'. The victory is clearly envisaged
and guaranteed, but the course must be run. What our
hearts have already reached, our bodies must struggle to
achieve. 'We must create in ourselves,' writes Joan Chittister,
'spiritual reservoirs that take us past every barrier in
church and state with peace in our hearts and calm in our

lives, knowing without doubt that the questions we ask are not of our own making only.'

> Once upon a time, the Zen masters say, an old woman made a pilgrimage to a far away mountain shrine during the worst part of the rainy season. Stopping at an inn along the way, she asked for a night's lodging before beginning her climb up the holy mountain. 'You'll never climb the slippery clay of that mountain in this weather,' the inn-keeper said, 'it's impossible.' 'Oh, that will be very simple,' the old woman replied, 'You see, sir, my heart has been there for years. It is now only a matter of taking my body there.'[2]

As we revisit the stirrings of our original vocation, does that story, many years or decades later, say anything to our present state of mind, of body, or of heart? Is there still a passionate vision that drives us onwards; and are we in the right place, with the tools we need, to work out that vision practically? Our satisfaction and joy in priesthood depends so much on the harmony we experience between these two dimensions of our ministry: between the passion and the practicalities, the vision and the tactics, the dream and the work demanded to bring it about. The highest form of Christian life, according to Thomas Aquinas, is not action or contemplation in themselves, but the graced ability to integrate the two patterns. In the structuring of the suggested models offered below, we have tried to keep some kind of balance in honour of both dimensions of our priestly ministry.

Re-visiting our vocation

To begin with, at some stage in our young lives, even though the reasons, with hindsight, may have been somewhat ambiguous, we really did hear a 'call': we felt we 'had a vocation'. This 'original vision', this deep desire to follow God's invitation to serve God's people, may well have been defined in terms of a mission to 'convert and save souls', usually through encouraging a more committed adherence on their part to the one, true church. Set in the context of past decades, there could be no other way. Our dreams and hopes will always search for a structure that is defined by the social and religious language and understanding of the milieu in which they happen. These holy aspirations are as true now as they were then, but the context has changed.

The question to be asked is whether that first God-given vocation can now be revisited, revised and revisioned in terms of a wider, catholic, ecumenical and more human and creation-centred context. Such a context would draw new boundaries. It would re-interpret 'conversion' and 'salvation' in terms of the human hearts that crave for a new meaning, an authentic freedom and a spiritual beauty in a world that has little to offer by way of nourishment for this hunger. It would be defined by Pope John Paul's desire for crafting a 'civilisation of love'. Its ground-plan would be drawn around what Cardinal Hume describes as 'the spiritual thirst of God's people today', a people in search of an alternative to the current, deceptive saturation of a relentless consumerism.

> Traditional evangelisation was the process of bringing the 'deposit of faith' into a foreign culture. This deposit was clear and clean in form and content. A native response which took it on, was termed a 'conversion'. Behind this whole process, and sustaining it, was an understanding of culture and theology which are now gone. Christian theology now recognises that the Catholic Church is not emperor of theological truth but that all churches and religions participate in different ways in the truth. Together with the loss of theological arrogance, there has been a loss of cult-

ural arrogance, namely a recognition of the autonomy and independence of local culture, a rediscovery and appreciation of their indigenous mythology and spirituality. The old authoritarian maxim 'Go teach all nations' has had to be radically qualified. Ironic- ally, western culture is now looking more and more to indigenous culture, and relearning from it the rhythms of a spirituality that we have lost. From this perspective, it seems that western culture in its frag- mentation, reductionism and spiritual hunger, needs evangelisation more than indigenous cultures.[3]

There is an inevitability about God's ways with us. While there is always a divine continuity and progression, it is not always obvious. To us, creatures in time and space, it can only be experienced in the context of endings and be- ginnings, of failures leading to growth, of a disillusion- ment hiding a new hope. Like the changing seasons that pass over our fields and our daily lives, there are seasons too that pass over our role as priests. Maybe, as well as being called to save and convert people into membership of the church, we are first called to the primary task of lib- erating people into the fullness of their own already- graced humanity, into revealing to people the blessedness of their very being, of their capacity for living the abun- dant life in the here and now.

Perhaps this is the place to address some comments made by fellow-priests on reading the first drafts of this book. 'Are the models,' they asked, 'seen through rose-tinted spectacles?' But are they? The living out of each model be- comes possible only through a dying of some kind or other. Jesus never promised a rose-garden to his followers. It is, inevitably, the way of the cross, a way of diminish- ment, a *via negativa*. A spirituality of diminishment implies that we will forever struggle with our own wayward hearts and with a world that lies to itself, calling itself free

yet enslaving millions, calling itself just yet imposing injustice on half the world, calling itself peace-loving yet
treating the voiceless with ruthless force.

> The spirituality of diminishment implies that we
> will go on without promise of success, with no
> memorials raised to our efforts, with no institutions
> to mark our accomplishments, with no respect for
> age, with no certainty that any one, at any time, will
> come behind us to complete the work ... Given the
> decline in our numbers, we excuse ourselves from
> the struggle. Or we become cynical about new ef-
> forts, new ideas. Or we deny the present situation
> entirely and settle down to wait for another age. It is
> a serious moment in the life of the soul ... The idea of
> starting over to do new work with new energy wear-
> ies us to the bone...

> But this is a great moment for those whose souls are
> still alive with God. Diminishment requires more life
> of us than we have ever known before. It leads us to
> be ourselves, to give everything we've got, to know
> the power of God at work in us, far beyond our own
> strength, far beyond our own vision. Diminishment
> gives us the opportunity, the reason, the mandate to
> examine our lives, to begin again, to dredge up what
> is best in us, to spill it recklessly across the canvas of
> the earth... Diminishment throws us back, whole and
> entire, small and trusting, aflame and afire, on God.
> And a life in God is anything but dead. It is glory be-
> yond glory beyond glory.[4]

Crisis or Opportunity

Fellow-priests have often asked me about the meaning of
this 'new' role, this vocation to call people into their true
selves, to fulfil their own graced potential for beauty, to
live more fully their own humanity, to grow through the
experience of the ubiquitous cross, and to realise their

God-given, barely-felt dream – a dream they still carry somewhere inside them. 'How can we,' they ask, 'be facilitators, architects and enablers of such huge strides of soul?' Many priests, when faced with this possibility, are open or fearful, interested or sceptical, excited or doubtful, eager or resistant. Such role definitions were not considered in our seminaries. Open though many priests may be to a new emphasis in their ministry, they still feel unprepared and therefore unable to be priests in parishes on such terms. Under the weight of current crises within the world at large, and within the church itself, the kind of priesthood to which they willingly gave their lives seems to be crumbling. Is it any wonder that so many priests, when they dare to face the inner truth of their lives, confess to a debilitating hopelessness? Fr Séamus Ryan expresses the feelings of many priests when he reflects on the decades of his life.

> There is an image from the gardening world which speaks with some power to my own life and my experience of priesthood over the latter third of this century. Even those with little gardening experience will be familiar with the pot-bound plant. The plant begins to wilt and wither. It has been in the container too long; the roots have nowhere to go, simply round and round inside the pot, eventually strangling and choking the plant. The roots are yearning to break out, to find more space, more soil, a new ambience in which to flourish and grow. After thirty-five years I have a sense of a priesthood that is pot-bound; too fearful to break out of the confinement imposed by the expectations of people who yearn for 'the security of familiar ground' and who would keep us 'pot-bound' in a style of ministry that is evidently no longer either effective or attractive.[5]

In recent years there are fewer and fewer priests pretending that all is well within the ranks of the clergy. Even the

more resistant of our members are lifting their heads from
the sand. The crisis is too near to ignore. At various stages
of desperation, priests are asking themselves some heart-
felt questions. (Yet there are, of course, many priests who
do not see themselves in terms of the following paragraph.)

> In the small hours and in the quiet moments, ques-
> tions surface about the wisdom of the whole enter-
> prise and our role in it. The field of dreams that
> opened out before us on ordination day is now a
> thicket we try to break through to preserve the ves-
> tiges of an ordinary life. What is left of me when so
> much is subsumed into priesthood? What is left
> when priesthood consumes the person I am? What
> can I do now to live a human life in the time God
> gives me? And the questions are forced back again
> into the recesses of the mind because in opening up
> the pain to the possibility, in speaking out 'our lonely
> thoughts in grey parishes', we remind ourselves
> about how precarious our grip is on the wreckage of
> our lives.[6]

But I truly believe that, with Jesus as our role-model, our
present Calvary can be pursued into our imminent Easter.
This timely, necessary invitation to shift the perception of our
role as priests, this urgent call for a transition in our awareness of the meaning of 'mission' and of being 'bringers of
the good news' to others, derives, in part, from the balancing dynamic of a re-emerging theology of creation – an understanding of revelation that honours the intrinsic goodness of all that God has made as well as acknowledging
the desperate need for redemption. This, in turn, requires
a demanding trust in the basic goodness of the human
heart. In the miracle of human birth, for instance, the 'in-
delible character' of the divine image, of the indwelling
Trinity, can never be forgotten in our roles as priests for
people. Long before the baptismal register is signed in the

required black ink, what a difference it has made to my ministry sometimes to catch glimpses of God's signature already written, with a lover's passion, across the small page of the baby's heart.

And so, when we as priests baptise these precious images of God, we are entrusting them to the Christian community of the Holy Spirit, to guide them and love them through a fallen world, so often gone astray in the pursuit of false gods and seductive idols. We are welcoming them into the family of Jesus, that safe place where love will always be their protection. I will never forget one Sunday, last Autumn, when I touched a sleeping baby's forehead, saying 'I claim you for Christ our Saviour by the sign of his cross.' A sudden smile spread across her perfect face. It was a smile of *recognition*. It was as though the sleeping baby already knew and was waiting for this to happen. Maybe in my old age I'm getting soft. All I know is that I will never forget that moment.

Too old To risk

Since most priests are in the second half of their lives, there is a huge temptation, especially in the face of current, threatening challenges, to 'throw in the towel', to quit the struggle, to surrender. 'I can't wait for retirement' is an honest expression heard so often these days. But are we ever too old to stop risking?

> Resignation now reigns where recklessness should be… (The priestly and religious life) channels every minute of a person's energy and vision toward a point beyond life itself and so never really arrives, never completes itself, never retires. For the religious (and for all of us) life is always beginning, never actually finishes, moves always toward the next moment of becoming. Death, of course, comes, but it does not come before every minute of life has been lived

to the fullest... There is always something important to begin at every stage of life, something new to learn, something important to give... The real truth is that old age is not the time to settle down at all. Not here. Not now. Old age is the time to try new things with abandon and imagination if life tomorrow is to be anything but a long, sad rehearsal of yesterdays far gone. To live until we die may, in the final analysis, be the ultimate goal of life.[7]

Some priests fret at a canon law that requires active service (where appropriate) until the age of 75. Allowing for many exceptions, maybe there is great wisdom in this seemingly demanding expectation. And maybe it is from the ranks of those of us who are over 50 that the renewal will begin. After all, we are the ones who have lived through an amazing few decades of changes in the church. After a fairly stable period around the time we were ordained, we encountered the *resurgamento* of Vatican II – a time when the windows were thrown open with great expectations – to be followed by the recent years of what many would call a climate of caution and retrenchement. To be 50, 60 or 70 is to be full of experience, full of wisdom and full of courage. The only thing wrong with these decades is to think that it means the beginning of the end. The experience of three such rich periods in the life of the church should only whet our apetite for another impending and inevitable evolution. At the very moment when the contemporary society, deeply trapped in its cult of ageism, expects decline in our credibility and in our very existence, the priesthood needs to reach deeply into its inner resources of inherited and hard-won wisdom and, after an exploration of its age-old meaning in the context of a postmodern world, emerge in renewed and exciting shapes. Our life now requires more a sense of risk, even of daring, than of caution and conformity. 'Religious life needs older members who refuse to give in to oldness of life and younger members who refuse to give in to oldness of soul.' One of Antony de Mello's stories is relevant here:

'Heavens, how you've aged!'
exclaimed the Master after
speaking with a boyhood friend.

'One cannot help growing old,
can one?' said the friend.

'No, one cannot,' agreed the
Master, 'but one must avoid
becoming aged.'

When we revisit our first feelings about 'becoming a priest', we will surely find a sense of excitement, of adventure, of uncertainty. But schooled from the start, as many of us were, in a seminary system where 'risk' was usually eclipsed by 'prudence' if not by fear, and then slotted into a parochial life-style where to be different was usually to be wrong, it is little wonder that, in a clerical atmosphere where the true sense of authority and obedience were often distorted and misunderstood, whatever seeds of courage, exploration and hope waiting in our young hearts were swiftly stifled, for so many before they had a chance to grow. But God took a huge risk in becoming a baby, and Jesus gambled with his life when he challenged the society and the religion of his day. I feel sure that at some stage of our early commitment to God, we had within us the same courage and trust that formed the hearts of people like Oscar Romero, Mother Teresa, Dorothy Day, Bede Griffith, Helder Camara and many other household names today. They knew something about risk.

Risk is not brazen talk by a warm fire on a dark night. Risk is not a virtue unless there is a high possibility of failure. It does not really exist until it requires something of us that at first sight, at least, seems to be almost certainly doomed to failure, yet it is absolutely essential to begin... The reporter who spends hundreds of hours of unpaid time to expose political fraud takes a risk. The theologians who admit that they differ with the magisterium in matters of debate take a risk in the interests of intellectual integrity. But they are not alone. Risk is of the essence of the integrated spiritual life.[8]

Common roles

A brief word about current work on the nature of one relevant aspect of priesthood may help to clarify the suggestions made here about the reason for, and the value of new models. The need for this consideration arises from the fact that, in many aspects, the models outlined here are common to all Christians. The issue is about the precise difference between the ministerial or hierarchical priesthood and the common priesthood of all the faithful. Quite apart from the almost unbelievable pastoral projection that early in the next century there will be about 1,000 priestless parishes out of 2,703 in the UK, the renewal of collaborative ministry in parishes, for instance, as an end in itself, is one of the main reasons behind the re-emergence of this debate. The current study of the meaning and implications of baptismal priesthood brings, in its wake, the need to examine the nature of the ordained priesthood more closely.

On the one hand, there has been a very real development in the role of the laity in the church and their collaboration with ordained priestly ministers. On the other hand, there has been a retrenchment in traditional models of priestly ministry by some, often undermining the newly found position of the laity or thwarting their work. Since the Second Vatican Council, the messages from the highest authority in the church concerning the nature and purpose of the ordained ministry and the role of the laity have been very mixed.[9]

Even before Vatican II, Yves Congar had pointed out (in 1954) that a proper theological treatment of this pressing need within the church, could only happen against the re-setting of a 'total ecclesiology'. Such work is only beginning. This, I suppose, is one way in which the development of doctrine happens, in the light of what the Spirit is saying to the churches at any particular time of need and move-ment in their unfolding self-awareness. I mention this wide-ranging theological and scriptural debate only to highlight one generally agreed point – that if there is an essen-tial difference between the ministerial priesthood and the common priesthood of all the faithful, it cannot be found in the word 'priesthood'. The late Fr Michael Richards takes up this theme:

> Priesthood is what is common to both sacraments – baptism and orders; a specific difference must be de-fined in some other way ... Over the centuries the church has slipped into the use of the term 'priest' in such a way as to obscure the radical (Christian scrip-tures) innovation which, on the one hand, made all Christians into worshippers (a role reserved to priests only in the Hebrew Scriptures), and, on the other, brought in a new type of representative or ser-vant of God, whose specific responsibility was to call together the church and provide all members with the means of becoming true priests in their daily life ... Fears that this way of understanding the sacra-ment of Order devalues sacrifice and, in particular, the Eucharist must be firmly set aside ... Bishops, presbyters and deacons gather us together now as a priestly people, each with their own way of being a priest, a worshipper, so that we all may be made whole, made real, by the presence of reality, the pres-ence of our great High Priest ...[10]

When people think of the priest, they tend to think immed-iately of the sacred actions which he alone in the parish is empowered to perform. As a result, they often see his role as a mainly liturgical one. This understanding is often held by people in a very tight and limited way. While the saying of Mass, the hearing of confessions and the anointing of the sick are always essential to the priest's ministry, and, as we try to show here, can flow out to touch, heal and reveal the holinesss of every aspect of human living, they are not the starting point for a definition of the role of the priest. No less an authority than Karl Rahner writes forcefully on the issue:

> This narrowly ritualistic interpretation of the specifically priestly task is not only humanly intolerable, but also theologically wrong, since it is contrary to a modern ecclesiology and to the history of the priesthood.

In his little classic on *Partnership in Parish*,[11] a book that explores the questions that may immediately arise in the mind of the reader, Enda Lyons looks to the scholars who agree that it is in terms of pastoral leadership – and not first of all in terms of liturgy – that the New Testament sees the priestly office. Edward Schillebeeckx, for example, holds that,

> Throughout the development of ministry in the New Testament, one striking fact is that ministry did not develop from and around the eucharist or the liturgy, but from the apostolic building up of the community...[12]

There is truly no need for alarm in our midst, in the light of such reflections. They are to be seen as invitations to pray about and study the origins and present realities of the unique priesthood we are privileged to share. The whole enterprise is too important to shelve for lack of nerve. Now is the acceptable time. Guided by the Holy Spirit, we have nothing to fear. But there are many questions. If, for instance, it is agreed among many current and concerned theologians that there is a need for renewed and additional

models of the ministerial priesthood of the future, even if
many of these models overlap with the role of all the baptised, against what background are they to be outlined?
Because we are all living in a time of amazing social and
personal change at every level, it is not easy to be sure-
footed in making any predictions about the future. All we
can do is exercise with discernment the gifts of prophecy
(as traditionally interpreted), and read the signs of these
pre-millennial years as best we can.

If we accept that the signs of the times point to the still-re-
sisted fact of a crisis within the ministerial priesthood, we
must surely search out some safe, true and proven foundations on which to build our new models and images. As
hinted at in the preceding pages, there are at least three to
hand. One concerns the rediscovery of a much-neglected
but orthodox theological underpinning that offers rich resources for this work. Another considers the well-attested
spiritual needs of God's people today, both as individuals
and as members of community. The third foundation lies
in the worldwide condition of poverty and oppression
(with the endless and awful realities and descriptions of
such conditions).

As a tentative attempt only, maybe it is in terms of this
backdrop that a beginning could be made. The following
images and models, then, of ordained priesthood, are built
mainly on these three foundations. (For a wider, more
comprehensive and more traditional basis for our reflections, see the Apostolic Exhortation *Pastores Dabo Vobis*,
1992. The document balances the priest's life of contemplation with his life of pastoral action, his call to be a mystic
with the call to be a shepherd. This balance is found and
maintained by the priest, as he strives, in his total humanity,
to be 'the living and transparent image of Christ the
priest'.)

The terms 'models' and 'ministries' are gaining much currency in literature about priesthood. While immensely helpful, they have their limitations too. Like all clarifying terms, they can be pressed too far. However, in *Priesthood Today: An Appraisal* (Paulist Press 1992), Thomas Rausch offers three models of priesthood that many have found useful. These are, the *sacral*, the *ministerial* and the *representational*. William Cosgrave critiques these in a two-part article in *Doctrine and Life* (*Models of Priesthood Today*, July/August and September 1997).

Readers will also be helped by Avery Dulles's theological reflection in *The Priestly Office* (Paulist Press 1997). In this small book, he outlines the roles and functions of priesthood in terms of three ministries – those of the Word, of Worship and of Pastoral Ministry. At a time of ambiguity about the future of our priesthood, I find these explorations of the meaning of our vocation, by acknowledged theologians, both enlightening and comforting. The contents of *New Hearts for New Models* are meant to bring a complimentary and personal dimension to such reflections about priesthood.

A new paradigm

a) Working, then, as much as possible within the structures of priesthood as we know it, the renewed models of priesthood offered in these pages, all presuppose a non-dualistic understanding of incarnation. By that is meant the exclusion of the fear-filled, sin-centred, punishment-based theories of redemption that still, in spite of our protests to the contrary, shape and colour so much of our teaching and preaching. There is a need to recover a traditional theology of creation in order to regain a lost balance in our interpretation of revelation. This need is underlined in Pope John Paul's Jubilee Letter *Tertio Millennio Adveniente*. A Christian theology of creation and incarnation holds strongly to the view that we co-create with God; that God

needs us to fill out what is missing in making divine redemption present amongst us today; that the self-empty-
ing of the Word confers on us the responsibility for liberating each other and the world from the greed called original sin.

After a fairly lean period in the recent history of Christian
theological development, a new dynamism is once again
beginning to colour our understanding of revelation. The
initial incarnation-centred insight of the early church
Fathers, continued in the churches' thinking in people
such as John Scotus Eriugena, Thomas Aquinas, the mystics of the Middle Ages, and more recently in the works of
theologians such as Teilhard de Chardin, Karl Rahner,
Edward Schillebeecks and others,[13] is gradually being re-
captured. Revelation is again seen as the amazing love-
story of God's desire to be intimately among us in human
form. Full of intense compassion, God wished to create out
of pure love and then, in time, to become that creation.
That becoming happened in Jesus Christ. In him it was revealed that God's heart beats in all our hearts, that all our
bodies are temples of the Holy Spirit, that every creature is
a divine work of art, and that original sin, even though a
felix culpa, carries the deadly seeds of awful destruction
and evil. (For a succinct scripture-based acknowledge-
ment of the balanced tension between a theology of creation
and a theology of redemption, read paragraph 22 of The
Pastoral Constitution on the Church in the Modern World,
Gaudium et Spes.)

Revelation is now seen to be about the beauty of being
human since humanity is the 'raw material', so to speak, of
God's presence in the world. Revelation is about the unbelievable possibilities of humanity, graced at its centre from
the very beginning, but flawed, too, throughout the history
of humanity. It is about God's desire to be known and
loved in the humanity of Jesus Christ. It is about God's de-

light in being visible and tangible in human form. This is how it became possible for God to be close to us, to share completely in the experiences of creatures, the fruit of God's own womb. We can say with saints and theologians from the time of Christ, that the incarnation happened, not just because creation went wrong at some early stage, but because in God's plan to share God's own divine joy with others, creation was first necessary so that incarnation could take place. To be true to this revelation entails our total commitment to co-redeeming, co-creating and co-operating with God, in Jesus, so as to make this divine vision a reality in our lives and in our world.

We remember the words of Jesus to St Teresa – 'I have no hands now but yours, no feet, no tongue, no eyes, to reach out, to comfort, to encourage, to heal my broken people...'. It is as though Jesus was placing the responsibility on her and on us to unfold and reveal the reign of God in our midst. Like midwives we are honoured with the task of bringing to birth the image of God in those around us. Michelangelo described his intention when working with his sculptures as releasing the angel from the block of marble. Priests and people are finding new hope in a traditional, liberating theology of revelation that is becoming increasingly accessible through the popularising work of our best theologians and communicators. Without the effort to be aware of, sensitive to, and, as far as possible, comfortable with such a dynamic theology – one which brings new life and meaning to our understanding of incarnation, of church, of sacrament – the models of priesthood outlined here will have little meaning. For priests who can spare a little time to read about such developments in christology, ecclesiology and sacramental theology, with significant implications for new approaches to evangelisation and mission, there are, as we have indicated in the references above, many useful and readable introductions to hand.

b) Michelangelo's revelations lead us into the second foundation for what follows. There is no denying the inner
hunger for spiritual values and personal renewal (not to
be confused with religious ones), that has emerged from
all the secular and church-sponsored polls and research
around Europe and the USA, at least during these momen-
tous, end-of-the-century years. The current exodus from mainstream churches indicates, amongst other reasons, a
deeply-felt lack of nourishment for people's soul-searching
in terms of healing, energising and growing. Cardinal
Hume indicates the holy locus of this yearning:

> Within each of us is an inner sanctuary, where none
> may enter save, perhaps, one or two close or trusted
> friends, allowed for a brief moment a quick, cursory
> glimpse of what is hidden within. It is our inner
> selves, often an area where we feel ill at ease. Here
> we experience suffering, that dreaded visitor, a thief
> that steals from us our peace of mind, our joy, our
> hope. Here too, however, we experience love, the
> guest that brings happiness and contentment. It is
> into this area – the inner sanctuary – that God seeks
> to enter and make his abode. Suffering and love are
> often, in different ways, the heralds of his arrival. He
> knocks at the door. We are free to open or not.[14]

If Cardinal Hume's assumptions about the state of our
souls are correct, if there is indeed what he describes as 'a
spiritual hunger' gnawing at out hearts, why does this
condition not bring in its wake, re-filling of our churches, a
return to religion? Maybe it is because the 'old' forms of religion seem incapable of bringing this hunger to articula-
tion in terms of its own needs and rhythms.

> One reason for this seems to be that the spiritual
> hunger is complex and highly nuanced. It is, in fact,
> a new and diverse form of consciousness. The old
> answers and methods of religion are stuck in a dif-

ferent idiom and cannot even meet or recognise this. Church documents, exhortations and so much of its preaching have the tonality of an earlier, more uni- form, authoritarian culture which modern con- sciousness has left behind long ago. Much of the language of religion is caught in this 'time warp'. It attempts to speak with the voice of a vanished age to a fragmented culture that has outgrown it.[15]

A contemporary role for the priest, imaged against this background, would see him as the one who first enables people to hear more clearly the voice of their own thirst, and then, who helps them understand that such an aware- ness and sensitivity is already stimulated by the action of grace in their souls from the beginning. Incarnation re- veals that it is within the current and ordinary that God's heartbeat is heard. St Teresa of Avila sees God as the one who strolls amongst the pots and pans of daily chores. Patrick Kavanagh finds God in the bits and pieces of each night and day. When taken seriously into our self-under- standing of our roles as priests, when the meaning of our regular sacramental celebrations are radically coloured by this revelation, then a sea-change takes place in what it means to be a Christian and in what it means to be a priest. We do not bring God to people because God is already walking in these people's shoes. The Good News we bring is through the delicate awakening of this awareness. 'Evangelisation is the good news that touches the origin, memory, identity and destiny of life itself.' A balancing theology of creation, intrinsically linked with a theology of redemption, provides the raw material for this second foundation.[16]

c) The third foundation for building some images and models of priesthood today is found in the unceasing op- pression of God's children, of the sisters and brothers of Jesus and, therefore, of our family too. This is a reality which racks the conscience of all concerned human beings, not just committed Christians and priests. The universal concern for a practical resolution to the plight of those who are called 'poor' in every real sense, is now raised to a priority for the Christian churches. In his Jubilee Letter, Pope John Paul writes, '...it has to be said that a commitment to justice and peace in a world like ours, marked by so many conflicts and intolerable social and economic injustices, is a necessary condition for the preparation and celebration of the Jubilee.'

At a time then, when millions of people across the earth, are busy signing 'covenants with the poor' with their hearts if not their hands, is it unreasonable that we, as priests, should not be at the forefront of such a divine mission? Is it not an intrinsic dimension of our very calling? At their annual meeting in Maynooth (1997) the Directors of Pastoral Formation in the Seminaries of England, Wales, Scotland and Ireland came to the following conclusion:

> The church derives its fundamental model of how to be in the world, from its presence among people on the margins. The sense of energy and purpose required for initiatives in pastoral formation for ministry in the church and to the world, are drawn from here.

(The implications are:)

> – that in being in the darkness and its confusions is a holy place to be, albeit an uncomfortable one;
>
> – that all those involved in ministerial formation, formators and students, can only benefit through being more aware of the darkness in their own lives;
>
> – that working alongside the marginalised is not an option but of the essence;
>
> – that we must earn the right to enter into the darkness with others;

– that it is only from the margins that the signs of the new growth of spring can be spotted and named.

Frank Regan reminds us about the cost of such discipleship. Even as we walk with 'those on the margins,' we need to be familiar, also, with the margins of our own inner territories, as Jesus was:

> But even as we say 'Here I am, Lord,' is it not also true that each of us should try to be acquainted with the faith-filled self-denying, that carries the seal of divine support?

> By emptying himself of his Godhead, Christ commits himself to a radical way of mission relationship. His self-emptying was the doorway to mission. As a result he could 'do mission' with empty hands... We are growing into an understanding that 'mission' is relating to people from a perspective of a similar faith. With empty hands, aware of our vulnerabilities, frailties and fears, we reach out...[17]

And on the heels of this commitment to all humanity, comes the responsibility of caring for the earth itself. This, too, is the body of God. As Catholics, we are not famous, at least in the present dispensation, for championing the environmental cause. But properly understood, a theology of incarnation, where all creation is believed to be the beloved child of God, though needing, to be sure, a fundamental purification arising from a condition of original sinfulness, can lead in no other direction.[18]

This issue is of particular and urgent immediacy at a time when our globe is now threatened by an environmental crisis of unprecedented proportions.

> It has often been argued that an excessive anthropocentrism (over-emphasis on the human dimension of our world) is the main source of our current environmental crises. An exaggerated focus on

human significance places value so heavily upon our own species that it thereby drains value away from the non-human aspects of nature. And this robbery leaves nature open to our own abuse. For this reason, our locating of revelation as a cosmic and not just an historical reality already has salutary environmental implications, for it counters the excessive anthropocentrism that has misshapen so much of Christian theology. God's gift of self is offered to the whole of the universe and not just to humans...[19]

It is only in the light of incarnation that the Christian can make all these observations with confidence. As the reader may be well aware, there is a huge 'paradigm shift' in what many of our more Christian physicists call the 'new cosmic story.'[20] It is mentioned here because, as priests, we need to be familiar with the implications of this amazing break-through in the scientific explorations of our times. The 'new story' calls for an urgent re-thinking and developing of much of our 'old' understanding of the mysteries of creation and incarnation, with a corresponding revisioning of our roles as priests.

The exciting dialogue will continue for many a day, as the secrets of the universe are revealed before our eyes. What needs to be glimpsed is the divinely revealed pattern of the oneness and intimacy of everything. For John and Paul, Jesus is the Wisdom referred to in the Hebrew scriptures, the centre of human and cosmic history. (Col 3:11; Eph 1:9-10) Wisdom is the artist who played with God in crafting the first creation. The same creative Word of God that is active in the beginning, is now the same creative Word that was made flesh in Jesus. And it is that Word that still urges humanity into the new evolution of human and cosmic compassion. (Jn 1:3-5)

Writing out of a theology of creation, Pope John Paul tries to bring ecological concerns to centre stage in the pastoral ministry of the churches. 'Christians in particular,' he forcefully reminds us, 'must realise that their responsibiity within creation, and their duty towards nature and its Creator, are an essential part of their faith.' (*Peace with God the Creator: Peace with all Creation*, 1 Jan 1990)

Some Discussion Points

1. How would you describe the crisis in our priesthood today? Is this crisis being adequately addressed by bishops and priests?

2. What do you consider to be the most hopeful aspects of our ministry? Can you imagine ways in which these aspects could be affirmed and developed within the church?

3. Do you agree with the author's emphasis on the need for an inner, spiritual renewal if we are to reclaim and recreate whatever dimensions of priesthood we may have lost in recent times? From where does our support come? Is there a way in which priests can offer each other such encouragement by open and honest debate?

PART II

Creating the Models

Models of Christian priesthood

The renewed models of priesthood are based on the notion of the priest as sacrament of the Word-Made-Flesh, as the living symbol of the inclusivity of the human and divine in Jesus Christ. In a renewed paradigm of priestly ministry, the emphasis is on interiority and the promotion of a radical awareness of true identity, source and destiny, rather than on an external functionality and a measurable achievement, necessary as these might be, but often best left to others who may be much better equipped for such ministries.

In what is traditionally called the *hypostatic union*, the humanity of Jesus – the primordial sacrament – unites the pleading Word of God, addressed to humankind, and the listening ear of the human race, ever open to hearing that Word. It is in that sense that the priest is entrusted with the deepest levels of sacramental intensity – levels that we predicate on, and that were focused in, the revelation that was Jesus. And when the priest is aware of his humanity as the key to his priesthood, as it was for Jesus, then a radical transformation must take place in his whole approach to his ministry. In a moment we will consider how clericalism is the very antithesis of this traditional Christian belief.

John O' Donoghue has written an article about the priestliness of the human heart.[1] In it, our attention is called to the spaces within us, which are so often overlooked. He begins by reminding us about the ambiguity, for the Christian, of what he calls 'the precarious and tender interim time' for today's church, when the old is not yet old enough to have died and the new is yet too young to have been born. It is a time when things beyond structures and strategies need to be explored. Through a crack in the disintegrating wall of the churches, during this decade of unprecedented revisioning, he points to a hidden vista of great beauty. In a letter to *The Tablet*, Fr Tom Grufferty writes, 'In terms of church history there is no vocations crisis. There is a crisis of vision to look once again into the treasure house. Our Catholic people are more resourceful and resilient than we think. There is a crisis of vision to turn a trend into a golden opportunity.'[2]

These reflections are among the reasons for offering some images of priesthood that might help us to re-vision our role as we approach 2000AD. There is little doubt that the following 'models' are very incomplete, inadequate and need much critiquing. Nevertheless, they are suggested with humility and confidence. For a beginning, holding on to the tried, trusted and powerfully effective models of priesthood that we already live, we add a few others. These are: the *farmer of hearts*, the *prophet of beauty*, the *healer of fear*, the *mid-wife of mystery*, the *soul-friend of community*, the *weaver of wholeness*, the *voice of the silent* and the *sacrament of compassion*. A few of the priests who have taken time to consider the appropriateness of these models found them to be 'tough going', commenting on their 'naïve optimism,' of their disregard for the 'blood, sweat and tears' of spiritual growing, and of their distance from where their own particular congregations 'are at'. Perhaps the reader can decide.

a) The farmer of hearts

Farmers I have known were well acquainted with their land. Given the right conditions, and with the help of sun and rain, they knew the potential of the soil. From their fields they drew a harvest of plenty as the seeds died and gave forth a hundredfold. And in the times of drought the occasional farmer 'with the gift' would divine, with his carefully-held twig, the hidden spring that waited a long way down, to be discovered and then run fresh and free to green the yellow earth and nourish its precious offspring.

The priest farms the field of dreams. He divines that underground spring, the secret spark in every heart. He knows that behind the veneer of our external lives, the eternal is at work. Within us there is a secret immensity that we seldom even glimpse. In its subtle wisdom, the eternal artist carefully designs a unique destiny for each person. 'Before I formed you in the womb...' To be born is to be chosen. There is a task that can only be accomplished by each particular heart. And this task of grounding, focussing and nourishing the creative longing of the divine within everyone, is priestly work.

Each life is urgent with divinity. There is nothing neutral in the divine. Its nature is creativity; its urgency is transfiguration. Each individual is made in the image and likeness of this divine creativity. This is where all human longing has its source. We are the expression of divine transfiguration. In each individual a different aspect of God finds form. To be spiritual is to incarnate and realise this new dimension of God. Each of us is born out of a different place in the circle of God's heart. This is the reason why each individual is unique: each comes from a different nest in the divine. It is towards this nest that our deepest longing tends; it is only here that the soul can discover her true poise and rhythm. To allow this to come through into the texture and fibre of our feeling, thought and action, is the task of faith. Much of our weariness and emptiness comes from our blindness to the secret divinity of our hearts. God is never

in competition with the human, rather the human is
the language of the divine.[3]

O'Donoghue argues for an organic kind of transfiguration
of our spiritual selves, rather than a forced change based
on dualistic models of creation and incarnation. This is
challenging stuff. The language and imagery may be unfa-
miliar to many, but full of meaning for others. Here is the
effort to dismantle the walls of a dualism that most of us
have imbibed with our mothers' milk. Given the fact of
original sin, the shadow of which is always our companion
along the journey of our souls, this dualism forever threat-
ens to poison the milk. It tempts us to draw a black and
white line between the sacred and the secular; it concedes
the higher ground to the holy over the human; it lives by
the divide between the things of heaven and of earth that
Jesus came to reconcile; it poisons the nourishment of
God's secret, disclosed to us in the incarnation of God's
own love into the recesses of our hearts, and forever indis-
tinguishable from them, like the water and the wine becoming one at the preparation of the eucharistic gifts. O'
Donoghue is pointing us towards the holiness and wholeness
of the seasons of our lives and of the human aspirations of
our souls. Nor is he blind to the reality of original sin and
of its all-pervading presence in the world we live in, acknowledging its infiltration into the human condition
from the beginning. And it is so consoling to know that the
soul, with its inbuilt discernment, and enlightened by the
sure light of our divine Revealer, is the true guide to its
own wells of wisdom and healing.

To testify to all of this is the calling of the priest. To witness
to the holiness of all life is his vocation. The counter-attraction
is not between the church and the world; it is between authentic and inauthentic ways of being human. Jesus, the
church, the sacraments, the priest, are all there, not to
draw people out of a neutral or even threatening world

into a safer, sacred institution, but to enable people, and all creation, to become aware of their inherent holiness and divine destiny. This growing awareness will change all our lives deeply. It will reveal the ignorance, blindness, greed, self-hatred and self-imposed limits that feed the alienation and dis-ease around us and within us, in an individualistic and consumeristic society. The priest's work, in the fields of life, in and out of season, is to reap a different harvest.

Readers of the draft manuscript for this book commented, as we saw, on the unwarranted optimism of a number of the models. They felt that the role of priest as farmer of hearts, for instance, was too easy – the seed grows while the farmer sleeps; and spring will come, invited or not. (Maybe they only ever lived on a farm during the halcyon days of a brief, childhood summer-holiday!) But ask a farmer about waiting for a long winter to be over; about watching the sudden rain destroy the hard-won crop; about loneliness and doubt when the nights are long and cold. The farmer knows something about the discipline of waiting, about the stature of trusting, about the perennial interplay of light and darkness, about the mystery of death and life. He knows that only if the seed in the ground first dies will there be a rich harvest; that the fresh and green new shoots can only grow from their winter-womb. It is for good reasons that St Paul draws on the hard reality of the farm and the farmer for images about the nature of working towards the reign of God in our midst. George Herbert's serene and unwavering trust in the seasons of salvation and in the redemptive power of God is beautifully expressed here:

   Who would have thought my shrivel'd heart
   Could have recovered greenness? It was gone
   Quite underground; as flowers depart
   To see their mother-root, when they have
   blown;

Where they together
All the hard weather,
Dead to the world, keep house unknown.

As *farmer of hearts* the priest is no stranger to the subtle influence of sin as well as to the stronger influence of divine
grace. This he will be aware of in the first place, as he
watches and feels the spiritual seasons of life pass over his
own soul. Like the farmer he will know that there is no 'instant harvest', that no one can 'force the river'. In the farm
of hearts, there is no short-cut to happiness, no cheap
grace to salvation.

But we are still trying to redraw the maps of our lives,
without the jungles of confusion; to reroute the traffic of
our rushing hearts, so as to avoid the rush-hour of painful
encounter, to reset the compasses of our souls, creating di-
versions around the deserts of empty and arid places. If
we only knew that in so doing, we are resisting the disguised highway to our deepest wishes. Scott Peck reminds
us that most of our neuroses arise from the avoidance of
necessary pain. Ernest Hemingway observes that while
life breaks all of us, some people grow at the broken
places. It is not the experience of hurt and hate and envy
that destroy us, but the refusal to acknowledge them, to
accept them, to encounter and dismantle them.

St Paul writes about taking care of the hidden self, about
setting it free by bringing the suppressed emotions to the
surface, about realising that what we thought was dead
and buried was, in fact, only buried, but not dead. All of
our buried emotions are buried alive. And how we resist
the call to come out into the light! How strong the attraction of the darkness! What fascination we carry for the destructive forces that are rampant in our deepest centre!

These paragraphs on the reality of the struggle that a
farmer of hearts must be ready for, could be repeated in dif-

ferent ways, for all the models presented here. They are offered because of the perennial and unfounded suspicion
that a theology of creation and a spirituality of the heart
pay insufficient attention to the awful reality of original
sin – that human condition which, according to the catechism
of our childhood schooling, 'darkens the understanding,
weakens the will and leaves in us a strong inclination to
evil'.

b) Prophet of beauty

There was once a sculptor working hard with his hammer
and chisel on a large block of marble. A little boy who was
watching him saw nothing more than large and small
pieces of stone falling away left and right. He had no idea
what was happening. But when the boy returned to the
studio a few weeks later, he saw, to his great surprise, a
large, powerful lion sitting in the place where the marble
block had stood. With much excitement the boy ran to the
sculptor and asked, 'Sir, tell me, how did you know that
there was a beautiful lion in the marble?'

We all carry a beautiful lion within us. Most of us are unaware of the lion's presence because no one told us he was
there, and anyway he is asleep. One of the tasks of the
priest is to remind us of the precious image inside us. This
work is 'the ministry of beauty'. Made as we are in God's
image, the priest asks why, in spite of the perennial distortion of that image, we are all not daily delighted at the
wonderful creation we carry in our hearts. He asks why
we are not moved by our own inner splendour, by the
bright divinity that makes us sons and daughters of God.
There is a deep joy in revealing to people their own beauty,
in discovering for them their royal lineage. It is difficult to
imagine a more delightful work.

It is not every day that we preach along these lines.
Sermons on beauty are not commonplace. And yet people

yearn for such nourishment to sustain them in a human condition that is subject to the ravages of original sin. When asked about his devotion to his art, you will remember, the artist said he was motivated by the desire to reveal the angel in the stone on which he was working. The priest too is dedicated to revealing to people the angel they unknowingly carry within. Irenaeus was talking about beauty when he said that the glory of God was the fully-alive human being. So was St Paul when he reminded us that 'our unveiled faces reflect like mirrors the brightness of the Lord, growing brighter and brighter as we are turned into the image that we reflect'. (2 Cor 3:18) And in the most wonderful words, Thomas Aquinas assures us that 'God is beauty itself, beautifying all things ... God puts into creatures, along with a kind of sheen, a reflection of God's own luminous ray, which is the fountain of all light'. (*De Divinis Nominibus*, n. 340) We are born for beauty. We hunger for it all our lives. It nourishes us; it delights us; it fills us with good energy. And above all, it is such a healing thing. (Readers in search of a thorough grounding in the foundation that supports this model of priesthood, will find it in the writings of Hans Urs von Balthasar, the 'theologian of beauty'.) In James Joyce's *A Portrait of the Artist as a Young Man*, the protagonist, Stephen Dedalus, is grasped by a vision of the beautiful and feels compelled to abandon everything in order to become a creator and mediator of beauty.[4]

In its most profound meaning, the priest believes that it is only beauty that will save the world. He is aware of the urgent need to recover our lost sense of this necessary grace. We are well tutored in the virtues of goodness and truth. But without their sister, beauty, that blessed trinity remains unbalanced. Today our parishioners are held to ransom by a counterfeit attraction, intensely and relentlessly imprinted into our subconscious minds, and beguiling the souls of young and old. Our preaching of the Beautiful Word will help people discern the false from the true, empowering them with the knowledge of their own creativity, their dignity and their glory. We all sorely need to be reminded about how pleased God is with us, how good we are, how extravagantly precious we are in God's eyes. We need to be told each Sunday about how beautiful we are – our hands for healing, our eyes for smiling, our words for redeeming, our bodies for loving, our hearts for intimacy, our souls for vision.

As the priest explores with his people the mystery of the incarnation and the wider meaning of the eucharistic celebration, a sense of utter wonder overwhelms the human mind and heart. God was delighted to become a human being and to stay intimately involved with humanity in bread and wine. And within each of us is the capacity to bring God forth as Mary and Jesus did. Our bodies, too, are temples of the Holy Spirit. This makes them beautiful beyond compare, to be reverenced and cherished as Thomas Aquinas reminds us. (*Summa Theologiae*, 11-11, q. 25, a. 5) The task of the priest is to convince the people of God that this is so. They carry within them God's dream. We empower each other to make that dream a reality.

The sculptor in the story believed, like Michelangelo did, that he was but discovering and revealing the hidden form already complete within the marble. Beyond function and organisation, the priest's privileged work today is to bring the Saviour to birth anew in the heart of each parishioner – to make those he serves more aware and proud of their uniqueness as co-creators with God of the loveliness and holiness of human affection, reconciliation and trust. They are lovely because they are God's human ways of becoming incarnate in our world of time and space. And we know this to be true, because it happened first in Jesus.

As the boy in the story discovered, the lion does not just

appear. It takes effort. The tough, resistant marble of our conditioning and programming does not easily surrender. It is part of the mystery of growing. Like wisdom does, the beautiful baby, too, makes a bloody and painful entrance. Without darkness there is no dawn and spring begins in winter. Original sin and original blessing are the twin conditions of our human becoming. And the beautiful thing must be carved out in the heart of the priest before he preaches to others about beauty. He must accept and meet the lion in himself before he can recognise the sleeping lion in those he is called to serve. In a world of viciousness and cruelty it is the love, trust and gentleness in himself that calls forth the deeply hidden echoes of these graces in others.

Only those who have travelled the barren journey of self-purification can continue to believe in the inner, abundant glory of someone else. The mustard seed of beauty must grow in the priest before it grows out, to take root in another heart. This, I think, is what it means to be a mystic. Priests are all called to be mystics, to be men who are at home to mystery. And only the mystics will survive. They are the people, according to Karl Rahner, who are absorbed in the mystery of life. They reflect and wonder at the richness of each experience, at the challenge of darkness, at the power of our hearts.[5]

Each priest is called to be a sacrament of the mystical, a reminder for people of their divine loveliness. He will need to meditate on the mystery of the incarnation which reveals the beauty of humanity even as it unfolds the beauty of God. There is a beautiful way of celebrating Eucharist, of preaching the word, of being present to the wounded, of being intimate with life, of walking like a child on our precious earth. And as the priest is more and more fully transformed in his own graced humanity into the image of God, then *every* meal and word he shares will be a small but vibrant sacrament of God's beauty, warming his people's hearts when they grow too cold, and bringing the morning early, when their nights are too dark and too slow.

> The beauty of the body of Christ in human bodies must be revealed most characteristically in the celebration of the eucharist. Some church designers claim that the only colour in the space where the eucharist is celebrated should be provided by the people … Maybe St Thomas' reference to 'bright colour' which he saw as an important aspect of beauty, could be a good starting point for describing a 'colourful' people. In the same context, maybe the statement that every eucharist should be a 'new appearance of the Risen Lord' is more than a nice figure of speech. And is there a more lovely description of ministerial priesthood than the 'ministry of transparency' that theologians have talked about and that the recent synod on priestly formation made its own?[6]

As *prophet of beauty*, the priest needs to be profoundly sensitive to the implications of the incarnation – when the beautiful Word became fallible flesh. This model of priesthood calls for a graced vigilance in discerning the presence of God's loveliness inextricably permeating the human condition in space and time. In his book *Art and the Beauty of God*, Bishop Richard Harries writes:

> One of the strengths of the Christian faith is the way it can hold together in one vision, the physical and the spiritual. The world has been created good and beautiful by God. Christ has claimed it as his own and will raise it to eternal light and life. This means that the material and the immaterial, the visible and the invisible, the physical and the spiritual interpenetrate one another. The physical world becomes radiant with eternity and eternity is seen in terms of a transfigured physical world. This means that all everyday experiences have a sacramental character.[7]

Among the many prophets in our midst who can discern this sacramental character of people's daily lives, surely the priest is in a privileged position to play a special role in such discernment. Familiar with the mystery of God's love incarnated in the humanity of Jesus – one who struggled like us, who failed like we do, who was tempted as we are – he carries, like one of God's spies, the charism of penetrating the divine disguise of the divine indwelling, even, and especially, in the most unexpected places.

> God's glory is revealed in humble, self-effacing lives of faith and love. It can be fully present in failure and ignominy. It is almost entirely a glory that is veiled … In the light of this, many of our standard notions of success and failure are radically reversed. Christ, the King of Glory, reigns from the tree … He reveals the divine glory because he is the truth of God and the love of God in human terms … As human beings we will always stand in a profound, puzzling, tensionful relationship to all forms of beauty. For the full glory of the world about us will be largely hidden in lives of secret self-sacrifice, of unceasing inner prayer, of profound artistic achievement that goes unrecognised in its own time. On the other hand, all that is fine and flourishing, all that is beautiful and radiant as God intends it to be, has its place in that transformed world which belongs first and foremost and finally to the poor and humble.[8]

One last comment about the priest as a *prophet of beauty*. There is a beauty in the single-mindedness of the priest who devotes the very best of his energy to his work. Most of us can number among our friends, priests who are unflagging in their unwavering attention to the people they serve. Whether it is constantly revealed in their unending and active sympathy and sensitivity to grieving individuals or families in their parishes, their capacity to rejoice with

the joyful, their remembrance of anniversaries, their antic-
ipation and accurate supply of the needs of others, their
commitment to the daily round of often-demanding visit-
ation, their instant availability in a small crisis, there is no
denying the element of a special beauty in this way of living.
It is beautiful when it is neither contrived nor pretentious,
when it is both honest and real.

Here, according to D. H. Lawrence, is a man 'in his wholeness wholly attending'. The title of Soren Kierkegaard's little classic is *Purity of Heart is to Will One Thing*. There is no
distraction in the priest's single eye as he struggles to be
worthy of his sometimes unrewarding service. A priest's
spirituality is very close to what he does all day. We are not
called to be supermen, to be ever-perfect, to be always sin-
less: we are called to be faithful. Neither are we called to
do extraordinary things in extraordinary ways but to do
little things well. This is what Mother Teresa meant when
she spoke about doing 'something beautiful for God' each
day. If beauty, then, has something to do with a never-ending sequence of small beginnings, if it is 'the product of
honest attention to the particular', then we have many
small epiphanies of beauty in the daily life of our parishes.

c) The healer of fear

Not every priest would readily recognise himself as a healer
of fear. We hold so much fear before the unknown, especially
before the unknown within ourselves. We need to recognise too that throughout history, fear has been used as an
agent of control and coercion by many groups and institu-
tions. To our shame, clericalism and authoritarianism
within the church has done the same. The ministry of the
priest, at heart, is about transcending and transforming
fear into the grace of love until, one day, God will be all in
all. It was by revealing to us our true nature that Jesus
overcame and harnessed for us the power of our fear.
Original sin is about our resistance to this revelation. Our

fear betrays the power we still concede to those threatening places within us. Writing these lines on Easter Monday morning, I believe that it was only fear itself that stayed nailed to the cross of Good Friday.

I'm sure it is true to say that the main role of the priest, like that of Jesus, is to dismantle the strange power of fear over our lives. When he listens in the Spirit, the priest is creating order out of the chaos of someone's depression. Pure, creative, compassionate listening is intense with spiritual energy. It is an imaginative interpretation of what is happening in someone's soul, or in our own, or in that of society. It is a deciphering of the drama of Jesus in the story of individuals and communities. It is a rewriting of the unfolding of our lives in the light of Holy Week.

By his contemplative presence to what he is doing, be that listening, preaching, celebrating or silence, the *healer of fear* is allowing the radical truth of each situation, no matter how contorted, complicated or contradictory it may seem, to emerge. This truth is sheer gift; it is a healing wisdom that brings clarity, order and peace to confused and tormented parishioners. It is the first grace of the Holy Spirit that ends our misery by naming our journey, thereby removing the ignorance, the root cause of fear. And in some mysterious way, this happens within the very person of the priest. He heals by absorbing into himself the jagged edges and broken bits of peoples' lives. It is in himself, like Jesus, that the priest reconciles all things. For those priests who endeavour to live out this model of ministry, it goes without saying that it is a recipe for the kind of breakthrough that brings crucifixion and passover in its wake.

Familiar with the anxiety that stalks the lives of most people at some time or other and, because of his pastoral experiences, highly sensitive to the precariousness of life at all times, the priest is a kind of doctor of souls. Under the microscope of faith, he identifies within the sick psyche traces of the health-giving strains implanted in each soul from the beginning. He reinterprets pain for those who live the life of quiet desperation. Living the Passover mystery himself, he uses pain to heal pain. In this sense he is a kind of alchemist, bringing spiritual gold out of the metals of suffering. He is like a recycler of experience, redesigning stumbling blocks into stepping stones, revealing the divine energy within the sacred wood of the cross.

Having personal evidence, at some critical moments of his life, of the soul-gift disguised under an infinite variety of negative experiences, the priest himself is no stranger to paradox. Immersed in the mysterious story of his Lord and Saviour, and weary from the cost of discipleship, there is immense graced power and confident authority in the way the priest is present to the broken heart. Intense with a burning faith in the divine ability of each soul to break through its walls of fear, the priest infuses his parishioners with a similar conviction. With Jesus as the model of such breakthrough, and with his own experiences of the light that is created at the point of his darkness, the priest is the walking sacrament of the invincibility of the faithful heart. Often bleeding himself, he moves among the people like a wounded doctor, a damaged healer, but also like a fiercely burning beacon of hope and faith that cannot but stir into life the tiny, almost snuffed-out spark of God in the hopeless soul.

Not everyone, however, allows their shadow to draw near enough to be recognised. It is here that the priest has such a crucial role to play. It is here that he prays with his people for an increase in their faith and courage. It is here that he reminds them that they can do all things in Christ; that though they should walk in the valley of death there is no evil to fear. And at this point of pain, in the here and now, the priest will emphasise that the moment of salvation, the fruits of redemption, the hard-won freedom for the children of God, is enfleshed and experienced by the individual, in time and space. From his pastoral presence, the priest can give many examples of that interface of disclosure, those moments of transcendence when the grace we carry by virtue of our birth and baptism erupts from within the fearful soul to flood the arid spirit. In the desert of the heart, let the healing fountain start.

In a leisure moment, Nobel Prize candidate, Piet Hein, scientist and philosopher, wrote this:

> The noble art of losing face
> may one day save the human race
> and turn it into eternal merit
> what weaker minds would call disgrace.

The priest will remind his people that whenever we consciously face loneliness and rejection, when we accept responsibility for our sins and destructive drives, when we refuse to give up despite immense pressure to call it a day, when we stay faithful to our vocations in spite of failure or betrayal by ourselves or others, when we are falsely accused and refrain from blaming, when we are struck down by failure, disgrace or diminishment and still trust, when we continue to believe in beauty in the face of ugliness and lies, when we forgive those who try to destroy us and seek reconciliation, when our broken hearts find new power – when any of these things happen to us, there, and there only, is the moment of truth. This is the timeless time when the saints are made. It is called the *via negativa* to God.

During these bright Easter days of 1997, let me offer a personal reflection. St Benedict's parish, where I currently work, is the gateway out of East Leeds into the beckoning plains that show off the proud city of York. Its big fields creep trustingly up to the increasing network of highways that run like the lines across an open palm, its finger pointing to the freedom of the northern dales. We are in an interim period between the demolition of our old church building and the completion of a new one.

A strong thread that holds us together in this wilderness of waiting is a beautiful bronze design specially commissioned to mark the opening of St Benedict's in 1967. It has an evocative motif, recreated in its many imaginative presentations throughout the original building. The most striking of these is a strange-looking cross over which we often meditate. It lets the light in through a big gash at its centre so we call it 'the cross of light'. It has cavernous spaces in its design, so we call it 'the empty cross'. But most of all, it is full of jagged pieces of flying splinters, so we call it 'the exploding cross'. It is as though the energy at its centre can contain itself no longer and must break free from its prison. Hence its power. In our farewell to our beloved place of worship, I wrote this meditation:

> It is at the point of pain that grace gathers at its highest intensity. Suffering has truly been called fuel for the spirit. This we know from the passion of Jesus. His Calvary darkness exploded into Easter light. Therefore all our suffering is redemptive too. When we unite our pain with his, small miracles happen.

> The tabernacle door (which carries the same motif) opens along the vertical line of the cross. Just as once in history, and far away, the stone was rolled from a certain tomb, to open the way for the saving Christ to come forth, so too, each Sunday morning, and in this very church, the opening tabernacle door splits the cross at its centre, to reveal within its shadow the bright Bread of Heaven.

I remember one Good Friday afternoon watching our parishioners remove their shoes and file slowly towards this very cross. One by one, young and old, they reverently pressed their lips, in a gesture of almost ultimate intimacy, against the cold comfort of this bronze symbol of pain. I was so moved at the mystery happening before me. I was astonished at the depth of a faith that could draw people into such a rich and profound ritual. How could they embrace this symbol of death? How could they kiss the very source of destruction? On this dark day, how amazing it was, how full of terror and beauty, of graced insight, of a trust that swept far beyond the boundaries of our earth-bound experiences, that we publicly and deliberately, mostly blindly yet hopefully, knelt down in adoration before the gaping wounds that destroyed our Saviour, and that are undoubtedly, at first perception, also destroying us? In *Oh God Why?*, Fr Gerard Hughes writes:

> Suffering, in itself, is an evil to be avoided. While it is true that some people are ennobled by suffering, the majority are diminished or destroyed by it. God's will for us, as scripture frequently says, is life, not destruction and death. Jesus did not will suffering; he prayed to escape from it. 'Father, if it be possible, let this cup pass me by.' He declared himself to be the fulfilment of Isaiah's prophecy – to bring good news, to proclaim liberty and vision and life ... But if we let God into our pain (even though this pain may well be self-inflicted, when our bruised ego is threatened by criticism, failure, rejection, etc.) and acknowledge its origin in our own expectations, and pray to be delivered from our own false securities, then the pain can become curative, leading us to freedom from our false attachments, and to the knowledge that he really is our rock, our refuge and strength, and that we have no other.

> ... Because if we are to be healed and transformed, we have to enter, with him, the pain of things. It is in our woundedness, not in our power, that we find him. He is a God who weeps in our hearts, but his tears are healing tears, springs of everlasting life,

cleansing, sustaining, giving hope when everything seems hopeless …[9]

d) The midwife of mystery

As all experienced priests, spiritual directors, prayer-guides, teachers and parents instinctively know, they do not heal people; they do not give to their visitors, children, pupils, something they already lack; they do not pour out from their own fulness something to fill the empty spaces of those around them: rather do they draw out from the hearts and souls of those they are privileged to serve, the innate wisdom and beauty and healing already waiting to be released.

In the context of the role of our teachers, I remember quoting the following verse many decades ago. I see these words today as equally relevant to the role of the priest. Just as with the process of education in general, so too with spiritual guidance in particular.

> Man may be taught perhaps only
> That which he already knows,
> For only in soil that is ready
> Grows the mind's obstinate rose.
> The right word at the wrong time
> Is wind-caught, blown away;
> And the most that the ages' sages'
> Wisdom and wit can say
> Is no more to the quickest pupil
> Than a midwife's delicate steady
> Fingers aiding and easing
> The thought half-born already.[10]

The priest is the *midwife of mystery*. Mystery has nothing to do with problems. Problems are there to be solved. Mystery is the backdrop to all our searching for knowledge and wisdom. This is so strikingly expressed in the first chapter of Ephesians. In it, 'mystery' is the womb of epiphany. It reveals God's plan for each one of us, and for the whole of creation, as a poem of love. The mystery in the heart of the eternal Creator is now made known; what the prophets longed to see, what the universe has waited for, what has been revealed to mere children ... Everyone is a bearer of this mystery, carrying the holy seeds of wisdom. Because of our birth and baptism, we are gifted from the beginning with the promise of this divine wisdom. The work of the priest, like the gardener, is to nourish these seeds into blossoms. Like the artist who looks at the marble and sees the hidden lion or angel, like the farmer who looks at his winter fields and sees a waving harvest, like Jesus who looked into the hearts of sinners and saw the face of his God, so too the priest looks at his people and sees the damaged but restorable handiwork of the Divine Artist.

Like the poet, the priest sees infinity in an hour, heaven in a pebble, eternity in a smile and divine power in a forgiving word. His vocation is to enable others to see everything that way too. This vision of the really real, this insight into the mystery of things, does not come easily to eyes that are forever clouded by the scales of original sin. There is a discipline to discipleship. The priest is called to educate and purify the flawed perceptions and attitudes of his people, so as to see the agony and ecstasy, the boredom and excitement, the failures and successes of their lives with the eyes of Jesus. He can only hope to achieve this miracle of grace if he, first, in his own life's experiences, travels this difficult but fascinating journey.

Only then can he provide a window on to the landscapes and horizons of the lives of his parishioners, so that the patterns and motivations, the gifts and the shadows of their days and nights, can emerge with a clarity that enables them to make a choice for light or darkness. This discernment of shallows and depths requires a certain kind of distance and objectivity on the part of the priest. A special space must be allowed for the movement of the Holy Spirit. Just as fishermen these days fly high in small aeroplanes over their fishing grounds to spot the deep and promising places for casting their nets down below into the rich shoals of fish, so too with the priest. He must first distance himself from the immediate condition of human confusion so as to be more accurate, in the Spirit, to move in, with a holy precision, to heal what is broken, to bring wholeness to what is divided.

People today are hostages to consumerism, racism, sexism and all kinds of elitism. They are tempted by the hidden persuaders of materialism and trapped by the empty logic of instant gratification. Young people, too, are relentlessly pursued and seduced by the empty promises and false values of greedy and powerful moguls. Where is the truth? Who is the prophet with the compass to guide a lost generation? Here, too, the priest is like the spiritual sleuth in search of life-giving clues in a place of confusion; the holy scout with eyes skinned for God's footsteps in a territory of misleading signs and ambiguous symbols; the ordained guide whose job it is to point out the safest way for pilgrims through the hills and valleys of their daily lives; a kind of miner who probes the packed soil of our complex existence for the gold that reveals the true source and destiny of our human condition. This is amazing work for the priest – to be God's spy in infiltrating the government of false gods until the true and hidden self of each human being is brought to light.

> Out of his infinite glory, may he give you the power through his Spirit for your hidden self to grow strong, so that Christ may live in your hearts through faith, and then, planted in love and built on love, you will, with all the saints, have strength to grasp the breadth and the length, the height and the depth until, knowing the love of Christ, which is be-

yond all knowledge, you are filled with the utter
fullness of God. (Eph 3:16-19)

It may help us as priests, at this point, to make a distinction between priesthood and priestliness. For many understandable reasons, priesthood can over-concern itself
with function, with doing things, with servicing, with mission (changing others into something different) or mainten-
ance (holding things as they are). While wonderful work is
accomplished under such interpretations of explicit priesthood, the notion of an implicit priestliness picks up a
deeper rhythm of transformation. Both understandings, in
fact, would ideally be harmonised into one melody. In the
article by John O'Donoghue, to which I have already paid
tribute, he writes:

> The intention of priesthood is not to bring people
> something which they lack and with which you have
> been exclusively gifted. Rather the priest attempts to
> kindle in them the recognition of who they are.
> Priesthood longs to awaken the who to its origin,
> presence, possibility and promise. In this way priest-
> hood attempts to awaken the fecundity of being to
> the possibilities of its own becoming. Consequently,
> priesthood is ministry to the deepest nature and
> identity of the person. It attempts to bring the hidden
> rhythm of our priestliness to awareness and realisation.
>
> In priesthood, priestliness becomes explicit as a
> commitment. A vocation to the priesthood is a call-
> ing to the realisation of one's own priestliness in the
> service of the implicit priestliness of all people. This
> vocation is akin to the vocation of the artist. An artist
> is called: there is a necessity and inevitability about
> the artistic vocation. The artist mediates the eternal
> through refined attention to the imagination.
> Without the presence of the imagination the eternal
> could never reach us. The imagination is the great

friend of the eternal. Imagination and divinity are sisters. As the sacrament of transfiguration, the eucharist is the source and summit of priestliness and priesthood. A priest is an artist of the eternal. However, when one works in the invisible world of soul, one may labour for years without seeing anything, and when something is finally disclosed it is usually in sign or glimpse form. The eternal is reserved, subtle and shy. When explicit priesthood denies the imagination it becomes functional and reduces itself to clericalism.[11]

The purpose here is to see 'priestliness' as one of the contexts of priesthood. One of the hopes expressed by the Directors of Pastoral Formation in the Seminaries of England, Wales, Scotland and Ireland, (1997) about priesthood today, was that individual priests might see themselves as 'effective expressions of the priestliness of all people'. This is not an easy thing to do, but it is a challenge for us during these 'years of turning' – at a time, for example, when priests and parishioners are embarking on a renewed collaborative approach to the meaning of being church. The quiet work of recognising the holiness of others, of 'soul-making', is so often and so sadly neglected in a world that rewards results. But if we persist in the roles that we are praised for playing, there is an ever-present danger of being trapped into over-action, measurable by tangible and visible results. There is an even greater risk of losing our freedom to serve, and eventually, our souls. We must, so to speak, collaborate within our own hearts before we collaborate within our own communities. Otherwise the action stays loveless; the music has no resonance; the emphasis is misplaced; the balance is askew; it is out of true.

e) Soul-friend of community

The role of the priest in the above models could generally be described as that of 'soul-friend'. This office of *anam-*

chara was held in exceptionally high regard among Celtic Christians. It is recorded in the *Book of Leinster* that St Brigid dismissed a monk who came to her for spiritual guidance, with the following advice: 'Go off and don't eat until you get a soul-friend, because anyone without a soul-friend is like a body without a head. The water of a limey well is not good to drink nor good for wishing. It is like a person without a soul-friend.' In *Mentoring: The Ministry of Spiritual Kinship*, Edward Sellner notes that this Celtic practice of being a spiritual sister or brother in Christ, is among the mentoring traditions currently being reclaimed in the USA, especially between men.[12] The writings of many mystics, psychologists, poets and theologians hold this ministry in very high regard.[13] John Henry Newman said that 'so much holiness is lost to the church because brothers refuse to share the secrets of their hearts one with another'. This great man had, as his cardinal's motto, *Cor ad cor loquitur*, 'Heart speaks to heart.'

The model of 'soul-friend', of *anam-chara*, recognises the truth that on our own, we cannot make much headway along the way to wholeness. 'In a straight line,' the Little Prince reminds us, 'nobody goes very far!' The *anam-chara* held the privileged and honoured position of the one who walked with the heart of another, not judging or condemning, not possessive or prescriptive. The soul-friend has access to the dark places within, is privy to the secret recesses of the inmost soul, whose first work is to help each one find their own truth. This work is about holding up the mirror to the true self of another, gently revealing the carefully concealed flaws and the strong, subtle veins of shadow that powerfully influence and control so much of what we say and do. There is no end, seemingly, to the tricks we come up with in our relationships with ourselves and others, the games people play in the serious business of living.

A number of the priests who have critiqued the drafts of

this book were uncomfortable with the (over)-emphasis on such heart-searching at a personal level and also, in the 'one-to-one' context. But I wonder about the validity of this feed-back. At a time of excessive, 'functional' demands on our time and energy, for all the reasons already referred to, maybe the general thrust of the models presented is not, in the end, all that unbalanced. For this surely is the foundation for the building of community. Just as the very church of believers to which we belong was first centred on the basis of a healing, integrating, personal and human friendship with Jesus, so too with the establishing and nurturing of the reign of God in our communities and parishes today.

There is no short-cut to a ready-made community. With the help of another, we must first befriend the many-faced, elusive members of the community of our own hearts before we start organising community on a wider front. 'To thine own self be true' is no easy advice. To realise that the kingdom of God is within takes much time and devoted attention. That is why all the models offered here are created out of such a daunting and deeply challenging call to personal spirituality. Too often we begin in the middle. We start the race halfway through. We embark on the outward-looking, activist part of our calling before examining our inward resources and energy so as to be sustained during the difficulties and conflicts that we must surely meet on the way.

What has led to the breakdown in the past of many promising and praise-worthy movements within the world and within the churches, is this reluctance and resistance to facing and exploring our own personal and spiritual integrity in the first place. Before the outer work can be entered into, the inner work must be underway. We develop and grow in a holistic way. Unless we are willing to risk the adventure of our own human development, and the challenge of relating to God through more intimate contact with another, with humanity and with nature it-self, we will become increasingly alienated from the new forms of Christian priesthood that are about to emerge.

To be sure, there is always the danger of being seduced by the 'cult of the individual' in an increasingly consumeristic world. Unknowingly, we become victims of the media's 'hidden persuaders', trapped and blinded in our political and religious options by the blinkers of personal gain. This temptation holds no less power in the politics of the spirit-ual. But once the fundamental option for personal, holistic healing and growing is taken within the context of 'the common good' and under the gathering, uniting energy of the family of the indwelling Blessed Trinity, we have every reason to hope that our desperately wayward, finite aspi-rations are in safe hands. What follows is an attempt to clarify this hope.

Richard Rohr writes with much authority on this issue, from his many years experience of building the New Jerusalem community. He traces the stages of community formation: the excitement of beginning and growing, the loss of heart when things fall apart, the confusion in the wilderness times, the persistent trust and faith that en-sures the ultimate harvest. Throughout the experiences of deepening the pastoral ministry of compassion in a parish, for instance, there must be the 'soul-friend', the spiritual guide, the listening leader – those who are familiar with these seasons in the year of their own hearts, who are ac-quainted with the deserts and oases in the pilgrimage of their own soul. Without personal exploration into one's own trusting and doubting, rising and dying, there will be no foundation on which to build anything.

> This inner journey into ever-deeper life is the essence of the faith community. It demands at least a few people who have made the journey on some level before. Some, or maybe just one, have to have

developed an eye for life and death. They will recognise some of the pitfalls, temptations, and traps
along the way ... And blessed are we if we have
(such) a true and wise friend to walk with us along
the dark way. We need someone who will not just
correct us, or just caress us, but who can say, 'I have
been here before.' We need the sister or the brother
who can assure us that there is light in this period
and not just darkness. Most difficult of all, we need
to have given them enough authority beforehand so
that we will believe what they say when nothing else
within us wants to believe it ... We need people who
understand darkness, and by their presence, can
hold us through to the light.[14]

This is the basis on which Rohr sees the emergence of true
community in parish or elsewhere. As the indwelling
Blessed Trinity within individuals is discovered and its
powerful graces released, then community has to happen.
The energy for creating and sustaining community in the
face of the destructive power of original sin, is generated
within the collaborating hearts of its members. Without
the 'soul-friend' of community, without the one carrying
this special ministry of listening, waiting and encouraging, without the healthily detached yet positively depen-
dent, spiritual guide, can God's people be gathered into
'family', can Lady Wisdom build herself a home? (Prov
9:1) It is at a time of huge decline in the practice of individual confession, and of an unprecedented increase in the
number of those seeking counselling, that this model of
soul-friend is a most appropriate role for the priest today.
Recently Laurence Freeman wrote in *The Furrow*:

At the present time, priests face not only the crisis of
numbers but, more pertinently, a crisis of identity,
role and inner life. The spiritual hunger of people
today points to a new role for the priest. He will no

longer fulfil his role only by celebrating the sacraments and administering the temporal goods of the parish ... deepest of all the critical questions today is the identity of the priest as a spiritual teacher or guide. (Jan 1996)

Given that we are here exploring a *charism*, and given that God is delightfully and confusingly free in choosing the (often unwilling or unlikely) recipients of divine extravagance, but given also, the present hierarchical structure of the church and parish, with the central, authoritative and spiritually significant leadership role of the priest and bishop, is it not reasonable to look, among other places, for the locus of this community-building service within the priesthood? The promised 'abundant life' cannot be introduced into a parish or group *en masse*. It must first take root and be carefully nurtured in each individual even as it becomes a dimension of community. Before the garden as a whole is thriving and healthy, each plant and flower must have, within it, the green sap of life. The experience of the struggle for individual fulfilment contains, within it, the imperative towards spreading and gathering. Those who are trustingly encountering the mystery of light and darkness in their own lives are irresistibly drawn to a divinely-implanted conviction – that the one thing that is more important than our own full life, is our own full life *together*.

The challenge of building community on truly spiritual foundations has always been acknowledged by most priests as being crucial to their ministry. In the society we find ourselves in today, this challenge is becoming extraordinarily difficult. There is an increasing sense of isolation around, arising from the break-down of many family and neighbourhood supports, with the inevitable consequences for parish communities. Where do we begin? The eucharistic gathering each Sunday, for instance, can all too

easily become a ritual devoid of any connection with current daily living, and without any sense of real community,
of coming together as 'one body'.

But it is here, precisely, that the priest, as president of the
gathered assembly, can seek to weave together the many
seemingly unconnecting threads that make up the one tap-
estry of that particular parish community. Often he is the
only person at Mass who can compassionately take in the
rich reality of the joys and sorrows that have been entrusted
to his care by those around him. When he faithfully tries to
reveal to people that in the blessed sacrament of bread and
wine, all of their lives and relationships are already holy,
already the body of Christ, then, as surely as spring follows winter, community begins to happen. This dynamic
leads to an ever-widening sense of church as 'sacrament of
healing' for the whole world.

The model of priest as *soul-friend of community* holds that
the work of 'soul-formation' in each individual is a prerequisite for the formation of community spirit, and that it is
the community itself that gives rise to and supports this
work from within its own members. There is a paradox
here in that there is a mutuality of dependence between
the individual and the community. But this is the interface
where the priest finds himself. Perhaps one sure way of
beginning lies in the fact that whenever people have
enough courage and trust to risk the 'baring of their soul'
to others who listen in an altruistic spirit of healing and
compassion, then grace flows beyond those concerned
and the community is enriched. The process is more involved in that we are challenged as individuals to expand
our souls, to become more and more aware of our own
limitations and the capacity we have for blocking as well
as for encouraging compassion and community.

Jean Vanier has spent a life-time of praying, working and

living in the L'Arche communities all over the world. He has no doubts about the necessary place of the inner journey by individuals in the forming of a wider family. His own spiritual journey into community began with his invitation to two men, Raphael and Philippe, to share his life. Community-living became possible for them, as it will for us, in learning the beautiful art of valuing each person we meet, calling out from them their unique gift, and drawing them into the larger family. Jesus also knew each person by heart, called each one by name, reconciled the differences and tensions among his followers, and in so doing, provided the world with a role-model for compassionate living and leadership. Can we, too, as priests today, trust that the time spent on the nurture of our own spiritual development and that of other individuals and small groups will bring about a vibrant community, conscious of its mission to the world?

Jean Vanier is ever aware of this vital, vibrant interplay between the inner work and the outer work. How many of us can identify our parish-communities in the following terms?

> Community is the place of forgiveness and celebration, growth and liberation. But when all is said and done, each of us, and in the deepest part of ourself, has to learn to accept our own essential solitude. Jesus is the master of community and it is his teaching which leads to the creation of Christian communities, founded in forgiveness and completed in celebration. But Jesus died abandoned by his friends, crucified on a cross, rejected by society, religious leaders and his own friends – and even by his God, 'Lord, Lord, why have you, too, forsaken me?'

> Community life is there not to help us flee from our deep wound, but to remain with the reality of love. It is there to help us believe that our illusions and egoism

will be gradually healed if we become nourishment for others. We are in community for each other, so that all of us can grow and uncover our wound, before the infinite, so that Jesus can manifest himself through it. But we can only accept our own deep wound when we have discovered where our heart can put down roots, a place where we are at home. The model of priest as shepherd, soul-friend, listener presupposes an understanding of the human heart. But he must also, and above all, understand the ways of God, and how the Holy Spirit, the master of love, is leading his people.[15]

If we are to deepen our understanding of our ministry as providing the service of a listening soul-friend, of being there for another or others so as to reconcile in ourselves, as Jesus did, the conflicts of lives in turmoil, it may well dismay us as a formidable task for which we are ill-prepared. It carries the promise or threat of much personal suffering. It is most certainly not to be entered into lightly. But Jesus assures us, from his unshakeable intimacy with his Father, that our joy will one day be complete.

Jesus lived out of ecstatic identity with God as his origin and sustaining energy. He was always receiving his 'self' from God ... In the canonical texts, Jesus implies qualities of humble service, love, empowered by his relation to himself, to the Father, to the indwelling Spirit, and to the community of faith. Given the many weaknesses of his disciples, he certainly did not imply moral and spiritual perfection as qualification (for this role of soul-friend.)[16]

Encouraged by such reassurances, today's priest is faced with the question, 'Is this one of the roles that I really want to take on?' Perhaps it has to do with exploring the direction of our hearts, with an emerging desire for this process to begin, with a strong trust that we only have to start in small ways, beginning with ourselves, and with courage and humility, and then, without anxiety, leaving what happens in the careful hands of the Holy Spirit. Tilden Edwards has the last word on this model. He sees a serious emphasis on the role of soul-friend and spiritual guide as necessary for the deepening of the community's life in Christ today.

> Both clergy and laity are forever in danger of sinking into functionary modes that cheat priest, people and community of authentic spiritual practice. The best place for priests to begin in this struggle is with themselves. Guidance for parish practice will emerge organically out of the pastor's deepening sensitivity to the Spirit's caring love moving in and through himself and the faith community. (*Weavings*, August 1987)

f) The weaver of wholeness

The image here is of the priest as a *weaver of wholeness*. To be a weaver of wholeness for others I must be always trying to weave a wholeness into my own life. The priest who is ready to work with this definition of his role must first look at the fractured reality of his own priesthood. This is notoriously threatening. It presupposes a courageous examination of the priest's personal and mostly secret thoughts and feelings. As an ordained priest, I find myself desperately resisting this challenge. It seems too much to ask of anyone. There is a part of me that I do not wish to explore. I have a part to play, a public role to fulfil. I have sins in my life that I dare not reveal. There is a cellar in my house that is out of bounds. Please don't ask me to go public with my vulnerability and weaknesses. I find it more comfortable to be a 'functioning cleric' rather than a 'transparent priest'. I have no doubt whatsoever that most of my brother priests have no difficulties with such distinctions. They truly are what they appear to be. They have honoured their promises and of poverty, chastity and obedience to the letter. But there must be some priest out there who feels like me!

Here again, we examine the currently accepted role of the priest with a view to its development and expansion in the context of the needs of individuals and of society in an unbelievably swiftly changing world. As well as his unique place in the sacramental celebration of eucharist and reconciliation, today's priest is called to provide other key ministries, offering a clear spiritual and pastoral leadership relevant to the unforeseen phenomenon of evolution at technological and many other levels, that most of us can barely cope with. Those other ministries are not to be understood as independent of, and detached from the priest's role as eucharistic president and agent of reconciliation. Rather are they to be seen as springing from them, focused on them and sustained by them.

As *weaver of wholeness*, the priest's function is *within* the Body of God's People, in the service of the reign of God, but not in charge of it. This function is not mainly administrative, organisational or even liturgical. It is about 'pastoral leadership'. In the parish which is a community of ministers there will be a variety of services requiring a variety of gifts. Such talents need to be recognised and developed. The priest notices, gathers, co-ordinates the God-given graces and potentialities of others. He is that part of the Body whose task it is to recognise, foster and promote the sacred dreams and energies of other parts of that same Body. He is called to inspire, to draw out, to draw upon and to draw together into one flow of power, the healing, saving ministry entrusted to every Christian by virtue of the incarnation and of the sacrament of baptism. I have recently heard a well-known theologian describe the priest as a 'kind of connector' – the live conductor of the various currents of life and energy around him, connecting the various gifted and broken bits of humanity into a healthy and vigorous body of worship and service again.

I have in my mind the picture of a conductor, skillfully creating a profound harmony from all kinds of instrumentalists and singers who happen to be gathered around the podium. They are giving birth to a tuneful melody. Because of the leader's trust in them, combined with a passionate love for every note and word, a new and lovely sound is pouring forth to refresh and gladden the hearts of all around. It is only the trained and pure ear that can discern and recognise the music within the cacophony of jarring thoughts and feelings. It is only the still and silent soul that can translate the noise of human experience, with all its discordance and false notes, into the song of God's score for humanity.

Father Tony de Mello, in his book *Song of the Bird*, has a brief tale entitled 'Music to the Deaf'. It is, I think, about someone who is present, without comprehension, to what is happening all around; someone who has the experience, but misses the meaning. Bishop Zipfel takes up the story. 'I used to be stone deaf. I would see people stand up and go through all kinds of gyrations. They called it dancing. It looked absurd to me – until one day I heard the music.'[17]

The priest is the one who searches for the rhythm that puts the dancing into the seemingly unconnected actions of people's lives. I have just pinned over my desk an advert from a newspaper (for motor-cars, I think.) It is a dense page of Beethoven's first edition of *Egmont*. Over it is written, 'It is just dots and lines and notes *until you play it.*' The priest, the *weaver of wholeness*, is the one who puts the cadences into the bits and pieces of daily life and celebrates their sacred meaning in the song of the eucharist. One of the revelations contained within the mystery of incarnation is traditionally expressed in terms of the surfacing of the meaning of our lives. Jesus reveals the significance of humanity, the preciousness of each moment of each day. Late last night I was again watching *Chariots of Fire*. In it, Eric Liddell, the athlete-turned-missionary, was trying to convince his fellow-evangelists of the divine immanence even in physical realities. 'I have been given a gift,' he pleaded, 'and when I run *I feel God's pleasure.*'

A Celtic story comes to mind. It is about the sacrament of the now. It is about not missing the only place that we can hear God's whisper of love to each one. It is about the precise moment when the curtain is drawn back and the love and meaning of our 'ordinary' experiences are revealed in all their splendour and glory. It goes like this:

> Once, as they rested on a chase, a debate arose among the Fianna-Finn as to what was the finest music in the world.
>
> 'Tell us that', said Fionn, turning to Oisin.
>
> 'The cuckoo calling from the tree that is highest in the hedge', cried his merry son.
>
> 'A good sound,' said Fionn. 'And Oscar,' he asked, 'what is to your mind the finest music?'
>
> 'The top of music is the ring of a spear on a shield,' cried the stout lad.
>
> 'It is a good sound,' said Fionn.
>
> And the other champions told their delight: the belling of a stag across the water, the baying of a tuneful pack of hounds heard in the distance, the song of a lark, the laughter of a gleeful girl, or the whisper of someone moved by love.
>
> 'They are good sounds all,' said Fionn.
>
> 'Tell us, chief,' one ventured, 'what do you think?'
>
> 'The music of what happens,' said great Fionn, 'that is the finest music in the world.'[18]

The *weaver of wholeness* is the one who hears and transcribes the music of what happens. He is the one who plays back to often-distracted people, the music of their lives. He is the one who puts together in a delightfully unexpected way, the fragments and splinters of a desperately disoriented sequence of lived experiences. He is the one who turns around the painfully-worked stitches and threads of a meaningless conglomeration of effort on the back of a fabric, to reveal to the jaded and bored artisan, a picture of rare quality and symmetry. He is the one who reassures people that the disparate jig-saw pieces of the stories of their lives can be put together into a life-transforming wholeness.

In his book *A Priesthood in Tune*, Thomas Lane points out that the vocation of all those who share in the priesthood of the one High Priest is to keep re-making, in him, the broken connections between earth and heaven. The one who is to proclaim the word at its highest level of sacramental intensity, is in a unique position to keep searching for ways to make the connections in word, sacrament, and pastoral ministry. He then offers a wide-ranging and wonderful summary of the role of the priest as 'connector'. (pp. 206-207)

Another way of putting this is that the priest-weaver helps people to see their lives against an infinite horizon. This horizon offers a rich backdrop of depth, a chamber of resonance, for the things we do each day. There is a story about the journalist who interviewed two men on the same building site about the nature of their work. One replied that he was bricklayer: the other said that he was a builder of cathedrals. Both worked with bricks on the same project. Their perception of what they were doing was so different! One teacher might say that she was teaching someone to read and write. Another might talk about co-creating with God a child of wonder, releasing within the pupil a divine wisdom and a unique beauty. The priest is the one who sees all things against an infinite horizon. The Jesuit theologian Walter Burghardt said that in life there is nothing secular except sin.

The weaver works with the raw material of human experience in time and space, in the here and now, and reveals the hidden design of eternity within them. He is like the membrane of the leaf that holds all together. He is like the web that reveals the wholeness in the discrete plans of many spider-like artisans. And like Jesus, the weaver's dedication and devotion is total. His life is his passion. Inspired by the Holy Spirit he is forever on the lookout for the divine love and meaning that is the infrastructure of our earthly existence. Within the mystery of the incarnation he lives and moves and has his being. He sees his vocation as facilitating the emergence and surfacing into human consciousness of the holiness of all creation, the recognising of God's unconditional love for us in the time-bound unfolding, not just of our own lives, but also of the life of the world and of the life of the whole cosmic mystery that is gradually revealing its secrets to us at this very time.

The many strands of community, then, which are in sore and constant need of weaving and re-weaving, are varied and widespread. And no matter how widespread they are, the thrust of this book is that we, as priests, must feel ourselves to be an intrinsic part of that creation-centred web. We can only accept our own woundedness when we have discovered that community is a safe place to call 'home.' This home-coming, this grounding of ourselves and our roots is not there simply to comfort us or to turn us in on ourselves, as so often happens. They are there so that each of us can grow and bear fruit for humanity, for the universe, and thus for God. Community is there not for itself, but for others – the poor, the church, society, and creation itself. It is essentially missionary. It has a message of hope to offer, and a love and a meaning to communicate to a distressed humanity and a despoiled environment. Community, therefore, will always have a political dimension.

So the *weaver of wholeness* has a wide brief. His role is lived out, not only among the members of his local community, but in the larger community of the neighbourhood of all those creatures who are 'groaning and waiting until God is all in all'. The woven web then becomes a place of reconciliation, where each person and every creature feels carried by the others and, in turn, carries them. It becomes a network of friendship and compassion for those who know that they are weak, but know too that they are loved and forgiven. Community is, therefore, a place of celebration.

Jean Vanier picks up on this reflection:

> Celebration is the sign that beyond all the sufferings, purifications and deaths, there is the eternal wedding-feast, the great celebration of life with God. It is the sign that there is a personal meeting which will fulfil us, that our thirst for the infinite will be slaked and that the wound of our loneliness will be healed. Our journey together, our universal pilgrimage, our world-wide weaving and our cosmic connections, are all worth while. There is hope.[19]

In our consideration of the priest as the weaver of wholeness, there is much more to be said. The wholeness of the individual, as we know, is only the beginning of the wholeness of society and then of all creation. The huge issues of universal freedom for people to live and worship according to their beliefs, to have equal rights and privileges in society, to live in an environment of peace and justice, to break through what Pope John Paul calls 'the culture of death' into a 'civilisation of love', must all be addressed by the priest-weaver.

I was sharing these thoughts with a friend of mine, Tony Cronshaw. Soon afterwards he sent me his reflections on 'Priesthood and Culture'. In them he traced the manner in which the dominant culture has influenced the role of the priest, and of faith itself, throughout the ages. There are volumes of church history that tell the grim story of the perennial capitulation of the clerical institution to the sovereign powers. Be that as it may, there are always priests whose inner spirit is made of stronger stuff.

> Oscar Romero is gunned down because, knowing the gospel of justice, repentance and reconciliation, he dares to proclaim a faith which will not be compromised by the threats or promises of the prevailing culture.

> Faith, stripped of bureaucracy, becomes the mirror through which the priest can evaluate the worth and value of the culture in which he exists. Being concerned, therefore, with the ultimate good of his fellow beings, the priest is conscience bound to strive for the gospel values in a world of dualism, individualism, pluralism, racism, sexism and all the other sinful 'isms' that the powers of darkness continue to let loose on creation, in a very materialistic society …
> But a 'paradigm shift' is happening all around us these years. The age of clericalism is dying because women and men have come to know in their hearts that bureaucracy and secularism have nothing to say about the true meaning of life.

(For an excellent summary of the present and future cultural context in which we are called to live out our faith and our various roles as priests, see Michael Paul Gallagher's *Clashing Symbols* (DLT 1997).)

Priests the world over are well aware of all these urgent issues; many are devoting their lives to eradicating the ills of society and to the healing of our world. There seems to be no end to the anxieties about how to restore to the oppressed of the world their basic, human dignity; how to ensure that national aid reaches the poorest people; how to open markets on fair terms to 'third world' imports and how to cancel unpayable debts; how to protect the genuine refugees and asylum seekers of the world from persecution, humiliation and landmines.

As *weaver of wholeness*, the priest will look towards *ritual* as a powerful ally in the weaving of this web of compassion. Good ritual can be the configuration, the constellation and the liberation of graced imagination. The priest is in a unique and blessed position for encouraging and creating such moving and effective liturgies. The unerring yearnings of our true hearts hunger for external form and expression. I experience it every week in our own parish school here in St Benedict's and at the workshops for adults offered by our Spirituality of the Heart teams. These experiences, even for the sceptics who occasionally muster up the courage to attend, are truly a God-send for our locked-up hearts. Working with dance and music, paint and clay, free writing and anointing with oil, all kinds of hidden hurts and suppressed and negative emotions are released before people find a safe, solid and lasting foothold for the rest of their lives. And what begins with a personal liberation will, with a divine inevitably, lead to wider horizons. Sean McDonagh, the Columban Fathers' environmental co-ordinator, pleads for new rituals that can help communities evolve a new mode of interaction with other human beings and with the natural world. Local churches and the Universal Church might imitate the Orthodox Church and institute a Feast of Creation.

> We have no liturgy to celebrate what Fr Thomas Berry calls 'cosmological moments of grace,' from the initial fire-ball, through vital cosmic and earth evolutions, such as the first stirrings of life, the first

blossoming of flora and fauna, and the appearance
of our own species. Liturgies like these would powerfully facilitate the reintroduction of Christians to the
old and 'new story' of creation. Even as it is, in the
Catholic liturgy there are many sacramental moments for the Christian community to experience the
presence of God in the world of nature. We are, for
instance, incorporated into the church through the
sacrament of baptism. The symbolism of life-giving
water and the power of the Spirit transforming the
lives of individuals and the whole community,
ought to act as a strong incentive for the Christian
community to ensure that their water and the waters
in their locality are not polluted with toxic, human,
industrial and agricultural waste. There are priests
who have refused to use the local water for baptism
because it was so grossly polluted.[20]

The eucharist, above all, is pregnant with all kinds of creative possibilities for deepening our awareness of the holy
communion which unites God, humankind and all creation. At Mass, the elements of bread and wine, taken from
the earth with its billions of years of evolution, and transformed by the creativity of human hands, are rich and
ready symbols for the explosion of an urgent and timely
revelation – a delightful yet awe-inspiring revelation
about the sacredness of matter, about creation as the expression of God's own being, about the evolution of our
cosmos, our world, our human condition and our personal
agonies and ecstasies as being now and forever, always
and everywhere, the Body and Blood of Christ.

The purpose of this book, however, is to focus on the inner
transformation of priests and people, and to re-emphasise
that the continuing work of social and ecological transformation can be achieved more effectively, more consistently
and more compassionately, with less lapses of nerve and

perseverance, less times of discouragement, when we 'begin with heart.' Our next two images of priesthood make more direct connections with the missionary imperative to save humanity and its homeland, the earth, spelt out with such shocking clarity in the Christian scriptures.

g) Voice of the silent

When we reflect on 'voice', on 'word', we come to a central dimension of priesthood – that of preaching. Keeping true to the underlying themes of this book – themes such as the interiority of the human person, the spirituality of the heart, the humanity of the priest – there are some points to be noted here. Peter Boucher writes that the renewal of the homily begins with the renewal of the preacher. When asked where to begin with this renewal of the preacher, Meister Eckhart, no mean homilist himself, replied, 'Begin with the heart.'

Such renewal will be both spiritual and theological. The Catholic bishops of the United States commissioned widespread surveys and audience analysis before writing a pastoral letter called *Fulfilled in Your Hearing*. They discovered that what people wanted most in preaching was simply to hear a person of faith speaking. We are not in competition with the slick presentation of the media. We are not struggling to 'think of something new to say' each Sunday morning. We are not expected to teach doctrines when we stand up to preach. What people want to hear, at least according to the research both in the USA and here in the UK (cf. Preacher of the Year Project, 1997) is the testimony of an ordinary man with an extraordinary trust in God. The love of God is caught, not taught. Only fire begets fire. Enthusiasm (being God-intoxicated) is contagious. This kind of emotion is not a clerical ego-trip. From the fulness of the heart the mouth speaks.

Robert Frost said that every poem begins with a lump in

the throat. Inspired preaching comes through inspired preachers who are not just intellectually but also spiritually and emotionally engaged with their message. Faith has as much to do with the heart as with the head, and much of our preaching has been too cerebral and intellectual. I can well recall the advice given to us in the seminary – 'keep *yourself* out of your sermons.' Many congregations would agree with this admonition! But a balance needs to be restored. Faith is a commitment that engages the whole person, heart, mind and body. Boucher explains:

> The human heart is hungry for the God who is love. Clever ideas about God will not satisfy the hunger. As one bishop at Vatican II said, 'What is needed now in our world and church is not an explanation of God, but an experience of God' ... Henri Nouwen puts it like this: '(Interior) availability is the primary condition for every dialogue that is to lead to redemptive insight. A preacher who is not willing to make his understanding of his own faith and doubt, anxiety and hope, fear and joy, available as a resource of recognition for others, can never expect to remove the obstacles which prevent the Word of God from bearing fruit.' Preachers need to live dangerously, to come out from behind the safety of written scripts, and risk the adventure of self-revelation which God initiated in Jesus, if they are to be dynamic instruments of the Holy Spirit... The whole exercise demands trust and humility on the part of the preacher who will be helped by realising that Christ is the real preacher and his own role is instrumental. Perhaps as preachers, teachers and writers, we all need to learn to get out of the way of the Holy Spirit who will lead us to the one Saviour Jesus Christ.[21]

Boucher then goes on to suggest that the writing out of sermons, at any stage, is a mistake. Priests I have talked with have strongly disagreed with this advice! Boucher claims, however, that while careful preparation is essential, and while most of us need some written notes to contribute to the 'planned spontaneity' of our homilies, the final, completed writing out of the homily destroys the necessary 'space' for the Holy Spirit, in its attentive freedom, to influence our words, and to catch the unique and subtle openness and readiness of a particular congregation, at a particular place and time.

These opening paragraphs on *the voice of the silent* as a title for a model of priesthood, are offered only to remind us that unless we explore the silent and hidden places of our own hearts first, we are hardly in a position to find much of an echo in the hearts of others. Whatever else our Sunday listeners may throw at us, they rarely accuse us of being 'too real, too authentic, or too sincere.' Whenever our homilies carry the resonances of the emotions of loss or hope, despair or delight, doubt or confidence, whether these be the silent stories of our own experiences or of those who have shared them with us, they are bound to strike a chord in other equally human lives. We can only walk humbly, attentively and confidently in the mysterious countryside of other people's lives to the extent that we have travelled fearfully, but hopefully, in the labyrinth of our own inner, silent spaces.

At the risk of being repetitive, this emphasis on such mutuality must always be made. Otherwise there is no power in the ministry of the priest. This unawareness of the microcosm/macrocosm image has led to the failure of many an excellent venture. When a passionate cause, for human or animal rights for instance, is pursued with too much detached ferocity and too little empathy and compassion, it can do more harm than good. This is as true for priests as for other 'prophets', protesters and lobbyists.

The interface between the inner and outer worlds is almost like a two-way mirror. To maintain a solid connection with the poor, the marginalised, the outcasts around us, we need to be always in touch with those within our own lives. We must always be trying to find and verify our own authentic 'voice' while we fulfil the role of being a voice for those who cannot, or will not, speak out their own truth. Richard Rohr puts it another way:

> I feel that the outer poverty, injustice and absurdity we see when we look around us mirrors our own inner poverty, injustice, absurdity. The poor man or woman outside is an invitation to the poor man or woman inside. As you learn compassion and sympathy for the brokenness of things, when you encounter the visible icon of the painful mystery in 'the little ones,' then, if you have built bridges between the inner and outer, if you have learned to move between action and contemplation, then you'll learn compassion and sympathy for the 'little one', the broken one within yourself. You'll realise that you are a poor person too.[22]

It is generally agreed, for instance, that across the face of humanity in the world today, a world of so much greed and inhumanity that Pope John Paul II has referred to it as carrying 'a culture of death', along with women and others, children too, are among the most persecuted and exploited feature of that face. A theology of incarnation invites us to reflect again on why God became a helpless, vulnerable child. Children are often a severely oppressed minority. Their innocence is relentlessly exploited. Yet there is something in God that can only be revealed in childhood. God did not become directly an adult to reveal the divine essence. Nor did God go through the preliminary stages of growing up just so as to reach adulthood when the real work of revelation would begin. God became 'child' because something of God's true nature could only be captured in the defencelessness of childhood. 'Of such is the kingdom of heaven' (Mt 19:14.) '...Jesus was neither more nor less the Son of God at the age of 20 or 30 than he was at the age of 6 days or 6 months. The Word was incarnated perfectly and fully in the child as child, just as in the adult as adult. And yet the child grew'. (British Council of Churches, *The Child in the Church*, Arts 34, 36) The suggestion here is that we can substitute for the category 'children' any group of people who come under the general term *'anawim'* – those treated unjustly and unequally, those who know no peace or freedom, those who cannot love because they receive no love.

Against the backdrop of this divine revelation we can begin to understand a little more clearly, why Jesus placed together the kingdom of childhood and the kingdom within; why he spoke, in the beatitudes, about the paradoxical blessedness for all who are open to grace, of those we tend to pity or cut off; why he told the mystifying story about saving ourselves even as we embrace and save the least of his sisters and brothers.

> The poor man's poverty at the soup kitchen is visible and extroverted; mine is invisible and interior. So the two sympathies and compassion connect and they become one world. I think that is why Jesus said we have to recognise Christ in the least of our brothers and sisters. It was for our redemption, our liberation, our healing. When we see it over there, we become freed in here, and we also become less judgmental. I can't hate the person on welfare because I'm on God's welfare. It all becomes one truth, and the inner and outer reflect one another.[23]

The *anawim* – the dispossessed, the refugees, the tortured, the lonely elderly, the disabled, the *special needs* children – force us to rethink some of our certainties about ourselves and about God. They can often be a *sign of contradiction,* unknowing prophets of the mystery of God. If God made nothing defective (Sir 42:24), then the *anawim*, in whatever way we wish to interpret that wide and rich range of people, show forth something of the splendour of their Maker. A true theology of creation and incarnation would celebrate that possibility. Such people safeguard the 'otherness' of God. They prevent us from fashioning God in our own image and likeness! They are part of the mystical *via negativa*, the way of unknowing that protects the mystery of the Godhead. God is different and always will be. And because of that we can never be too sure anymore about what we mean by the term 'normal'. Toward the end of *The Clowns of God*, Morris West envisages a poignant scene where God replies to the questions of some anxious, well-intentioned people about a seriously disabled girl in their midst.

> I know what you are thinking. You need a sign. What better one could I give you than to make this little one whole and new? I could do it; but I will not. I gave this mite a gift I denied to all of you – eternal innocence. To you she looks imperfect, but to me she is flawless, like the bud that dies unopened or the fledgling that falls from the nest – She will never destroy – She will remind you every day that I am who I am, that my ways are not yours, and that the smallest dust-mote whirled in darkest space does not fall out of my hand. I have chosen you. You have not chosen me. This little one is my sign to you. Treasure her.[24]

As we strive to gather accurately the silence of the empty and the waiting, into the words of our voice, as compassion and sympathy flow out of us to the poor and to the outcast, wounds are bandaged – both others' and our own. We'll never bandage them all, nor do we need to, but, as priests, we do need to get close to the wounds – not just read, study or pray about them.

The church has mostly tried to resolve all theological dilemmas with analysis and academic thinking. It just does not work. It produces a faith that is not real, that has no passion in it, no reality, no power to compel – just endless theological distinctions and books and articles, while the world goes by and asks 'Who cares?' This would not have happened if we'd kept Jesus' counsel to stay close to the poor. The poor kept us close to the gospels, to the important questions and issues, to the Christ-child within and without.[25]

There are two main aspects to our model of the priest as *voice of the silent*. One concerns the importance of the priest's ability to recognise and link his own inner poverty in his compassionate interaction with those others who are poor either in a 'third world' context or in a house two streets away from the presbytery; the other is about the context of community in which this priestly two-way ministry happens. It is 'two-way', as we have seen, because in the commerce of grace, it is the giver who receives, and it is the generous, humble, insecure and openly-needy receiver who truly gives. People who keep company with the marginalised, in whatever context, are constantly reminded of the real truth that we, mainstream church members, desperately need such close contact to reveal our own poverty. Such closeness discloses our elusive pride, our often-unknown prejudices, our crippling fear of those who are different, our subtle need, arising from very low self-esteem, for the power of always being the giver, and our patterns of operating, more deeply-seated than we think, a role of double-standards. As *voice of the silent*, how can we speak one word of truth unless its resonance and quality is verified and purified through such personal and painful revelation?

Those who come close to the poor do so first of all in

a generous desire to help them and bring them relief. But once in contact with them, once touching them, once establishing a loving and trusting relationship with them, the mystery reveals itself. At the heart of their insecurity there is a presence of Jesus. And the 'helpers' discover the sacrament of the poor and enter the mystery of compassion ... The poor man or woman has a mysterious power; in their weakness they are able to open the hardened hearts and reveal the sources of living water within them. It is the tiny hand of the fearless child that can slip through the bars of our ego-prisons.[26]

Without the attempt, by individuals, couples and small groups, to be always living-out this paradoxical and mysterious reality, there will be no divine spring of power to drive a community, a church, and assembly into a new age of God's reign. And without the supporting, encompassing and forgiving community to bless and grace the fearful, searching, often-despairing efforts of individuals and small groups, they would quickly lose heart and lose hope. Richard Rohr draws a distinction between a Leviticus-type church and an Exodus one.

When the clergy and ceremony take over and fail to keep that solidarity with the poor, then the Book of Leviticus takes over. We become too much concerned with laws and liturgies, structure, ceremony and rubric, with what goes on inside the church building. But most church does not happen best inside the church. The Exodus Church, on the other hand, is the church on a journey with the poor, busy encountering history, the outer world, liberation from slavery, the church as lifestyle and action, meeting along the way a much more gutsy God...[27]

A Christian community constantly calls its members to share, welcome, become poorer and go beyond their resources to a truer love. For that reason, a Christian community will always be a stumbling block, a question mark and a source of unease for society. The people around it will very quickly feel challenged and often confused. It does not make any 'normal' kind of sense to bypass the achieving high-flyer and to place the weak at the centre, to de-select the strongest team in favour of the most precarious and vulnerable one, to build community, not on the solid rock of tried and trusted righteousness but on the rejected and broken corner-stone of damaged lives.

> One of the most precious gifts in a community is to be found among the people who cannot assume important responsibilities. They have no ability to organise, inspire, look ahead or command. But they have very sensitive and loving hearts. They can straight away recognise people in difficulty, and with a smile, a look, a word, make these people feel that they are close to them, carrying their cross with them. The poor are always prophetic. As true prophets always point out, they reveal God's design. That is why we should take time to listen to them. And that means staying near them, because they speak quietly and infrequently; they are afraid to speak out, they lack confidence in themselves, because they have been oppressed and broken. But if we listen to them, they will bring us back to the essential. These 'insignificant' people are at the heart of the community and carry its extremes as well. It is the love of the hidden people which keeps the community united. The leader brings unity through justice; but these loving people are creators of unity just by being who they are. In their tenderness, they are artisans of peace.[28]

h) *The sacrament of compassion*

If people were asked, after reading through the gospels, to

find one word for the kind of person Jesus was, many would choose 'compassionate'. His compassionate heart seemed to inform his life. 'And Jesus, seeing the crowds, was moved with compassion.' (Mt 9:36) This profound adjective has depths of meaning, combining the finest elements of caring, of selfless service, of sensitive attention, and of true openness, humility and self-discipline. It is about the grace of love, stripped to its radical essential. It is about self-giving purified of self-interest. And for us priests, it is about the grace of a high degree of self-knowledge and self-awareness. It is a long struggle for us to see ourselves as not above, not in charge of, not even alongside, but as an intrinsic part, with all the accompanying pain and glory, of all humanity and of the whole universe. There is no short-cut to being a *sacrament of compassion*. Compassion springs from an awareness of the connectedness of every aspect of creation and life. It has to do with a sense of identity with all forms of existence. It has deep roots in the heart of the Creator.

When God becomes visible, tangible and available on this earth the result is incarnate compassion. We look to Jesus to see the face of God. The word, a self-portrait by the Creator, is drawn with the lines of compassion. Throughout the gospels, even when the word itself is not used, we can feel the movement of this instinctive gut-reaction. In Greek the movement of compassion means a deep-seated impulse that comes from the very bowels of the human being. Matthew quotes Jesus as saying, 'Don't be afraid', 'Don't be worried', 'Don't cry', and Mark points out that he was more moved by the last penny of the poor widow freely given into the temple treasury than by the grandeur of the Temple itself; and that while everyone else was so excited about the raising of Jairus' daughter, Jesus was more concerned that she should be given something to eat.

To fulfil his role as a *sacrament of compassion*, the priest is called to be the embodiment of divine mercy, the prophet of God's unconditional love. It presumes, in so far as we dare to presume, an acquaintance with with God's intentions, as revealed in Jesus, the Christ. The prophet shares not only in God's knowledge, but is filled to the brim with God's own feelings and emotions. For Jesus, it was God's essential compassion that possessed and drove him; he was its actual embodiment.

> All his convictions, his faith and hope were expressions of this fundamental experience. If God is compassionate, then goodness will triumph over evil, the impossible will happen and there is hope for mankind ... Compassion is the basis of truth. The experience of compassion is the experience of suffering or feeling with someone. To suffer or feel with humanity, nature and God is to be in tune with rhythms and impulses of life. This is also the experience of solidarity with each person, with each part of creation and with God. It excludes every form of alienation and discrimination. It makes a person at one with reality and therefore true and authentic within the self ... This made Jesus a uniquely liberated man, uniquely courageous, fearless, independent, hopeful and truthful.[29]

As *sacrament of compassion*, the priest too is called to embody God's extravagant love, first towards himself, then towards others and ultimately towards the entire universe. He tries, however falteringly, to reconcile in himself, like Jesus did, the sins and pain of the world with the limitless forgiveness and understanding of God. That is why compassion is no soft option. It is, in fact, an intensely-felt way of dying. It destroys suffering only by *suffering with and on behalf of* those who suffer. A Buddhist prayer is to use suffering so as to end suffering. A sympathy with the poor that is unwilling to share their sufferings would be a useless emotion. One cannot share the blessings of the victims of our inhumanity (the *anawim*) unless one is willing to enter into their painful plight as honestly and realistically as possible. And that is what priests, and all Christians, are called to do. Jesus wasn't just compassion incarnate, he also said to his followers, 'Be compassionate as your Father is compassionate'. This calls for the most sublime graces of trusting in, and letting go into, the ever-present, all-pervasive loving providence of our tremendous lover.

In his *Commentary on the Psalms*, Thomas Aquinas writes, 'We find these two things, compassion and justice, in all the works of God. Through compassion human beings imitate God … since God is compassion itself.' He reminds us that we know from the life of the Incarnate Word, how 'divine compassion has no measurement … it is the greatest of the mysteries of God'. (*Com. on Isaiah* 2, p 439) Notice that the Angelic Doctor links compassion with justice. This model of priesthood is about the transformation of people's attitudes especially in matters of equality and justice, peace and freedom. Lived compassion is built on these pragmatic dimensions of active ministry or else it dissolves into empty sentimentality. And justice without compassion can be too severe, peace without justice can be utterly false, freedom without responsibility can become wanton licence.

Compassion, as we have seen, springs from the intimate inter-relationship of all things. God's compassion becomes a little more understandable, then, when we realise that all creation, and every aspect of it, is the fruit of God's womb. God sees the divine Self in everyone and every thing. Only when we, too, see and know and feel the oneness of our universal sisterhood and brotherhood, can we 'suffer with' in an authentic and saving way. Only when we feel an intimacy with the elements of nature, with the turning of the seasons, with the pulse of the earth, can we passionately desire what Aquinas calls 'the common good'. No less than in the preceding models of priesthood, this role of sacramental compassion calls for the deepest letting go of the proud ego, of the subtle power-drive, of the imperative to control, of the compulsion to self-protection.

Compassion moves outwards. It will not be trapped into individual soul-saving. It grows only when given away and it can only happen in community. It is a 'reaching out' kind of virtue that is forever purified in the sharing. And it enriches the giver, because there is a sense in which our redeeming compassion is directed towards ourselves. We are a part of everything and everything is a part of us. This is another glimpse of the amazing revelation of incarnation. 'Blessed are the compassionate for they themselves shall attain compassion,' writes Matthew, and Aquinas comments, 'To be compassionate is to have a heart that suffers from the misfortune of others because we think of it as our own.' (*Com. on Matthew* 5, p 52)

We asked Donal Lucey, a local priest-friend of ours, and a sensitive guardian-angel to the *anawim*, especially to those who are 'different from the norm,' who find no place in the exam-oriented stream of current, competitive educational standards, who are gifted and handicapped with their own 'special needs', to tell us about his understanding of ministry in terms of a compassionate God. This is what he said:

Along the way, ministry became a success story. There were bonfires at the crossroads when we were ordained in the late sixties. But priesthood was never meant to be a success story. Our brief is in the area of prophecy. God has always sent prophets to speak to the needs of the age. The prophets do not add more noise to the predictable frequencies of their time; they are fine-tuned voices that call people to the deeper, if not spectacular, issues of life.

The spectacular belongs to the areas of sport and business. And that world is geared to what is big and sensational, to what is strong and powerful. But

not everything in life is big and strong and sensational. And maybe what makes the deepest impression on us, what is most valuable, are not the spectacular things, but the little things that take place between the great scenes of life. Henry Nouwen speaks
of the role of the clowns between the big scenes of
the circus – they relax us, they remove the tension.

We, as priests, are working between the great scenes
in the circus (and tragedy) of life. We are called to be
with people, to rejoice with them, to walk with them,
to stay with them, to suffer with them, to be the embodiment of God's compassion for them. In this
busy world, the priest is the one who has time (and if
he hasn't, maybe he should look at how he uses his
time!) The world is full of experts who interpret the
money markets for us, and our business career
prospects. But we are here to interpret the mysteries
of life for the community – when, for instance, a
child is born, and this may mean being a sacrament
of compassion when, for instance, a Downs Syndrome
baby arrives; when people fall in love and get married and, even more traumatic, when they fall out of
it and get divorced; when people die and their loved
ones are inconsolable. The priest, the agent of compassion, is there to unravel the dilemmas of illness
and disability, those deep issues that often happen
between the major events of life's relentless and urgent
unfolding.

Donal Lucey's reflections about finding the heart of compassion in the quality of our attention to the special moments in the lives of 'the little people', reminded me of
something in one of our parish newsletters written during
the last Olympics. It was offered as a meditation on the
current Sunday's gospel (Mt 25) about the divine presence
in the least, most marginalised and most ignored of God's
precious people. It gives an example from 'ordinary' life,

of how we, priests, within the graced opportunities that come our way, can also be embodiments of God's compassion for ourselves and for others. What follows is an extract. (You might consider it for your parish bulletin during the next Olympics in 2000AD, DV!)

In today's Sports Pages we will read about the fastest but not about the most patient; about the highest but not about the most humble; about the strongest but not about the most vulnerable; about the fittest but not about the wisest; about the most competitive but not about the most compassionate; about the glory but not about the cross. There will be many photos of the daring body-beautiful athletes whose amazing feats enshrine their names in the record-books of sport; you won't, however, find pictures of the fragile body-broken victims of needless violence whose quiet courage carves out their names forever in the Book of Life.

Fr Colm Kilcoyne, a parish priest at Knock, Co Mayo, tells the following story. 'In the middle of the Olympic Games a few years ago, a radio reflection was given by a nurse who began her talk by referring to the excitement of the games. She painted pictures of the triumph of the winners as they stood on the podium, with their medals round their necks and the roar of the crowd in their ears. Then she shifted the scene to the children's hospital where she worked. She talked about a child and a nurse. This child was very sick. He had serious bone trouble in his legs and couldn't walk. For months the nurse had worked patiently with him, trying to get the power into the frail little legs. She was also coaxing courage into his frightened little heart. One day she had him balanced yet again, on his supports. She pleaded with him, she loved him, she willed him into taking a step. He did – ONE STEP. She looked

up from his flushed, excited face to see a runner on
the telly, pump the air in triumph as he stood on the
victory stand – a full stadium and a world television
audience sharing his glory. There was nobody to
witness the boy's victory but his nurse. His little step
had been as great as the giant stride of the athlete.
Yet no cameras, no medals. Just a boy who had taken
one step and then fallen into the arms of the nurse
who wouldn't trade that moment for all the gold in
Los Angeles.

While all Christians are called to be channels of incarnat-
ing God's compassion, the priest especially is charged
with this ministry of service. We live in a world of frenetic
compulsions to relentless immediacy and highly-profiled
results. In this same world, too, there are moments of intense loss, grief, and desperation. But qualities such as pat-
ience, perseverance, faithful care, trusting encouragement
and hopeful waiting, are in short supply. In every parish
there are daily personal traumas arising from the sudden
news of severe illness, job-loss, infidelity and death. Such
awful moments strike indiscriminately and with deadly
regularity, bringing a desperate sense of panic and hopelessness with them.

Due to a lack of financial support, and therefore of person-
nel and necessary time, the normal medical, religious and
other social welfare systems are usually inadequate and
fairly helpless in the face of such intense, intimate and tot-
ally unforeseen tragedies. Such are the moments when
community-compassion comes alive. Such are the moments when the kindness of the neighbours comes up
trumps. And such are the moments when the parish
priests, the priests of the people, by virtue of their ordained priesthood, bring a special grace of comfort and
consolation to suffering hearts, devoid of masks and de-
fences, open, like moist sand when the tide has gone out,

to every impression of true love, sensitive understanding and total compassion. While in no way denying or papering-over the searing and bitter cracks in a tormented life, but instead, by being present to such pain with all the graced and resonating humanity that a priest can manage, there is always the blessed possibility of a slow breakthrough for the broken heart, into a new and life-giving spiritual ground – a break-through that in true Christian ministry is called 'soul-making'.

True to all the models offered here, the priest as *sacrament of compassion* will try to follow the example of Jesus, the sacrament of God. But speaking of God as 'compassionate' carries immense implications for many of the 'classic' characteristics we attribute to God – qualities such as 'immutability' and 'impassibility' (the impossibility of suffering change).

To hold that God is compassionate is to imply that God suffers with us; that God still suffers. There is an inadequacy in this traditional assertion of divine impassability towards the world. Because God is pure relation. To state that, is to state that God is in communion with the world. This kind of relationship of real love is always reciprocal. And God's relationship with the world is always one of true love. Does this love entail suffering in God? Yes, in so far as love always includes an openness to the other. Love includes a vulnerability to the other. It includes an empathy and a solidarity with the loved-one.

We have often 'traditionally' understood God as living 'out there', somewhere beyond and transcendent. To be sure, God has all these attributes; but God is also immanent, and nearer to us than the marrow of our bones. The letter to the Hebrews images the presence of God in the most intimate of terms, piercing the innermost places of heart and spirit, exploring bone-joints and marrow, closer than our own hearts. (Heb 4:12) A God in love with creation cannot be unfeeling or apathetic, but a passionate, suffering God. Our God, obsessed with an unconditional and extravagant desire for us, cannot be a mere spectator.

This is surely at the core of our understanding of God – a God in communion – a God who suffers when we suffer – a God who absorbs and reconciles within the divine essence, the pain of each heart and of the whole world. Because God's intimacy with us is an ever-lasting covenant, the divine vulnerability is not confined to the once-for-all broken body of Jesus on the cross. The Passover of our Saviour is the sacrament of the unending and ever-present compassion of God. God's omnipotence and God's all-embracing love come together in paradox, in dialectic and in mystery. And they are always revealed and available in Jesus as sacrament of God, in the church as sacrament of Jesus, and in each priest's ministry, in his role as the sacrament of the compassion of the sacred, human heart of the Blessed Trinity.[30]

Some Discussion Points

1. What is your reaction to the models of priesthood in the book? If you find yourself resisting them, or agreeing with them, do you know why? Are there ways in which the foundations on which they are built, and their emphasis on the need for a deepening of personal spirituality, could be better expressed?

2. Which of the models do you feel most comfortable with? Do any of them reflect your own understanding of priesthood in the situation we find ourselves in today?

3. What models are missing? Given that many current official guidelines for our ministry are presented in terms of 'models,' what would your own list look like?

PART III

Working from where we are

Priesthood and clericalism

We have looked at several possible images of priesthood today. For those drawn to such models of priestly ministry there are many difficulties ahead. What is it that prevents so many priests from moving into a new paradigm of their ministry, from finding a deep joy in their priesthood? Among the many obstacles that prevent this feeling of joy there is one, in particular, that militates against such satisfaction and fulfilment. It is clericalism. The above images belong to priesthood, but not to clericalism.

As with many of the issues looked at in these pages – issues so close to the very meaning of our lives as priests – there is a great danger of offering an unbalanced and unfair overview. In the following rather severe quotations, I do not wish to suggest that clericalism is inevitable in ecclesiastical structures, or endemic to the priesthood. There is, obviously, so much good to be said about the necessary reality of 'church as institution,' about the *presbyterate* as an identifiable and divinely ordained ministry within it, about the formation-role of our seminaries, and about the Canon Law that protects us all. Clericalism, like 'dualism' (see above) is a distortion waiting to happen within all ecclesiastical structures.

But clericalism, nevertheless, is seen today by many as the enemy of a mystical spirit, of a spirituality of the heart, of a focusing on the humanity of the priest, and of many other truly pastoral ministries. Yet, until recently, I have not seen clericalism even mentioned in articles or books, much less found it analysed, debated, held up to the light of the gospel. In a hard-hitting article, Colm Kilcoyne writes:

> Our church is now being asked to look inwards in-stead of outwards, to talk about its own faults rather than the sins of the world. It is being dragged, kick-ing, to face the enemy within. That enemy, I suggest, is an evil called clericalism. Clericalism is a caste sys-tem. It is self-righteous and self-perpetuating. It feeds off a sense of God-given superiority. There are Us and Them. It sees enemies everywhere. It has a lay, associate membership. Clericalism is good at black-listing. It resents having to explain itself. Clericalism is heavily into power. It may cloak its face in piosity but it is essentially a control system. It is ill at ease when it has to talk ordinary talk to ordi-nary people. As a caste system, it rewards servility, no matter how ordinary, and punishes independ-ence, no matter how loyal. It pushes to the margins those who will not burn incense. Inevitably, the stock weakens and the inbreeding finishes up with the potential for disaster of a royal family.[1]

Colm Kilcoyne holds that clericalism acts like a dysfunc-tional family. It rejects its failures. This reveals the caste-mind reacting to trouble in the ranks. What is being said is that those priests who fail to live up to their promises do not really belong to Us. But they *do* belong to the family, he insists. They *are* one of Us. We should not try to disown the weak. If we do, we disown part of ourselves. It is a ploy of clericalism to load the troublemaker with all the guilt and take the focus off possible flaws in the institution.

Not everyone will agree with such a forthright denuncia-tion. Many will feel threatened by this outspoken condemn-ation of a system in which nearly all of us find ourselves. But there is, I feel sure, the ground for a healthy debate here. There is little to lose by an open exploration of the pros and cons. And there is nothing to be gained by a blind defence of the status quo. If the focus is on the truth, pursued in a spirit of love and prayer, what is there to fear? John O'Donoghue opens up another window on to this sensitive issue.

A cleric is someone who attempts to be a priest from the outside in. He assumes and adopts the uniform, behaviour and language of the institution. Ultimately even his perception and thought become institutionalised. The role creeps deeper and deeper inwards until it houses at the heart of his identity. This can only be described as a tragic takeover of individual identity by an external and anonymous system. The tentacle structure of the seminary reaches down even to the presbytery and parish structure. In this way the cleric is insulated against the longings and possibilities of his own humanity. This isolates him from the humanity of others; he keeps himself out of reach in a limbo within the metallic surface of the role. The clerical role subsumes the complexity, conflict and depth of individual interiority. It offers no context or language which is hospitable to the intimacy, doubt or sexuality of the individual. Consequently, these are driven underground and often surface in addictive or twisted form.

Often it may be years later before he realises how much was secretly stolen from him in the name of an ideal that could have been realised in a more creative and human way. When role subsumes the natural rhythm of identity, it is no wonder that so much of clerical life is governed by fear. This fear keeps many lovely people confused and unsure, marooned on lonesome ledges in their lives. They usually opt to go along with things, even though their instinct is to disagree profoundly; subtle mechanisms of control

keep them silent and ensure that they will never
raise the awkward or wounded question.[2]

There is, I suppose, little hope of an immediate solution to
the issues raised in this emerging debate. On the one side
there will be the temptation to denial, to batten down the
hatches and let this storm blow over; to defend, to blame,
to ridicule the alarmists. On the other side are those who
are convinced of the need today for a searing honesty, a
humiliating vulnerability, a prophetic word of truth that
can only bring some kind of crucifixion. For all of these
reasons, and many more, being a priest today is complex
and difficult.

It is perhaps more especially poignant at a time when the
up-to-now unquestioned value of our 'compulsory celibacy'
is under review. How well I remember the title of an article
by Charles Davis, the priest-theologian, in one of our
Catholic journals during the mid-sixties. It was called
Celibacy – The False Sacrifice. I only mention this now because I know it is a huge issue for many priests today. But
we know, by heart, that *we really were called* and that *we
really did respond*. Yet there is little choice on this issue for
the one who feels so called and who did respond. But there
is something we *can* do about the choice we made. This is
priesthood at a time of crisis. It is therefore a precarious
time. We can either curse the darkness that seems to be de-
scending on us or we can search for a small light to help us
recover our original vision of commitment. Change is always a challenge. This little book is offered to those who
feel strong shadows, as a small candle to light the way into
another dawn.

The role and model of the ordained priestly minister
cannot but change profoundly over the coming
years. It will change not least because, as there will
be fewer priests than parishes, the priest will have to
work in partnership with lay-led parishes, and in

many ways, he will need to treat their lay leadership as just as competent as his own, and in some areas more so ... Plainly there is a creative theological ferment in the church at the moment. What is clear is that numerous models and patterns of ordained ministry, and indeed other ministries, are not only possible, but are now essential. They are essential if the demands both of maintaining the church and also of enabling it to be truly eucharistic and evangelising are to be met. The irony is that the official policy of retrenchment with regard to the models of ordained ministry is itself likely to exacerbate the crisis and to precipitate just such changes. The tragedy is that the price of these policies in terms of the increasing alienation of lay people and burn-out of priests could be unacceptably high. However, the agenda has been set and is fairly clearly spelt out: the church now needs the courage to devise the patterns of ministry which will promote its implementation.[3]

At this point, many priest-readers may be feeling uneasy or angry at the tone of the previous paragraphs. Here, too, some of those who read the first drafts of this book were irritated at the attack on clericalism. Confusing the condition of 'being clerics' with 'clericalism', they felt that their initial commitment and fidelity to the church was being called into question. But maybe this issue must be more thoroughly explored than it has been up to now. Understandable as our initial resistance may be to what may well emerge as an 'over-kill' on clericalism, there is too much at stake to set the debate aside too soon. A 'Family Workshop' director, familiar with many priests and religious caught up in the condition of clericalism, has this to say:

What I have found over the years is that clericalism, for many, is an addictive way of life. An addiction 'is any substance or process that has taken over our lives and over which we are powerless'. It can be a process that begins to have control over us to the point where we are not willing to give it up in order to make our lives fuller. In fact, it exerts so much control over us that we cannot see those who speak of its reality ... Sadly these addictive attributes contribute to the deterioration of the system and the people who make it up. I have seen many priests wonder why there was little or no spiritual growth available to them as clerics. As the years passed they often found themselves becoming more spiritually indebted and nearly spiritually bankrupt. They even spoke of having the sense of losing their souls. For those who see the addictive nature of the system and move in the direction of recovery, this is not the case. Their ability to mature, to respond to the graces to minister and grow and develop in their priesthood, is greatly enhanced. They are better able to resist the virus of low morale and disenchantment that is prevalent among the clergy today. [4]

The writers quoted in this section of the book are urgent and hard-hitting. Are they right in their convictions? Is there even a grain of truth in what they say? We address this debate only because it has immense repercussions for our freedom to pursue the possibility of creating new models for our lives as human beings and as priests.

These pre-millennial years, for us priests, are a kind of *Kairos* moment. In the New Testament, the word 'Kairos' denotes a special crisis-opportunity which challenges people and calls them to conversion. While this book is nothing other than a few gathered notes about the spiritual condition and possibilities of being a priest today, its wider aims are about recovering the lost place of ourselves and of our church, as sign and sacrament for the total well-being of

the whole world. The self-protection mentality of clericalism and institutionalism, its obsession with preserving an
impeccable outward face to deny its desperate fallibility,
can close our eyes, as priests, to the real, urgent and God-
given mission for the church and for the world today.
Helen Lombard, a Benedictine sister, in her address to the
Canadian Conference for Religious, had this to say:

> Just over two years ago, an event took place in my
> country (Australia) that was regarded as a signifi-
> cant event in the history of our nation. It was called a
> National Ideas Summit. You might describe it as a
> 'think-fest' – a festival of thinking. The most emi-
> nent, representative group of persons from across
> our nation was brought together, summoned by par-
> liament, to imagine what our society might be like,
> to dream dreams and share visions, to envisage al-
> ternative ways of ordering our society, to re-imagine
> our reality – in their language to imagine different
> 'scenarios' …
>
> This National Ideas Summit was held without one
> person being invited in the name of religion, gospel
> or church. We, whom Christ has commissioned to be
> grace for society, to be world-makers, to call our
> world to alternative consciousness, to an alternative
> 'scenario' shaped by the coming of his kingdom –
> we were not even within the horizon of choice.
> Could there be a more terrible or damning indict-
> ment of us, as witnesses and disciples? Could there
> be a clearer expression of what Pope Paul VI called
> the tragedy of our time, the complete split between
> the gospel and culture? (*Evangelii Nuntiandi* 20) Here
> there is no direct rejection of Christ and the values of
> his kingdom, no questioning of what these values
> might contribute to the meaning of human existence,
> to the issues of our time: they are totally, completely
> and simply irrelevant, so 'incredible' has our witness

become. How then in this modern world in which
we, as priests, live, to which we are sent forth and
into which we are called to walk with purposeful in-
tent, called to speak with the conviction and passion
of Peter (Acts 4.)? How is this world to be brought
into contact with the living power of the gospel?
Where is the cutting edge, where the gospel meets
the cultural situation, where sparks fly, conversion
takes place and newness begins? ...

If we live within the safety of a privatised discipleship, speaking the narrow language of churchspeak,
the modern world will shape its destiny at its national
and global ideas summits, arms summits, refugee
summits, migration summits, housing summits, nu-
clear proliferation treaty summits, environment summits, peace summits – and we will not be there.

Across the world these days, when local, secular organisa-
tions, national governments and international councils are
preparing for spectacular, creative and prophetic celebrations to usher in a new millennium, how strange it would
be if we, the carriers of God's intentions for the future of
our planet, for one reason or another, 'would not be there'!
The reason for our absence from such pivotal moments of
hope-filled decision and enterprise, many would hold, is
because we 'are not there' in the first place for our own ec-
clesial break-through at home; because we 'are not there'
as prophets for others at a threshold-time in our own communities; because we 'are not there' as confident midwives protecting and facilitating the tentative and mysterious 'Holy Saturday' moment that happens just before another resurrection for God's people.

However, instead of being agents of brave, new beginnings, we priests, according to Brendan Hoban, are actually
a dead weight on progress. In a devastating critique of the
status quo (*The Furrow*, August, 1997), he writes:

> One of the best kept secrets of the years since the
> Council has been the power of the clergy and the
> stranglehold they have on the church ... In those
> thirty years, priests have effectively operated a
> blocking mechanism to the emergence of a more ef-
> fective infrastructure for the church at local level.
> The reaction of the bishops has been in the main to
> accept the reality of a priests' veto. Defeated by
> priests in a series of skirmishes and convinced of
> their own inability to dictate progress, bishops have
> simply lost their nerve. (p 411)

Even though Brendan Hoban goes on to offer a number of
feasible options for unblocking the clerical log-jam, so that
a new and more collaborative flow may emerge, I find his
assessment of the current situation very depressing. Is it a
true assessment? Can we be objective enough, even while
we understandably want to defend ourselves, to verify or
deny its accuracy? Painful, distressing and even acrimon-
ious as this kind of debate may be, it cannot be avoided.
The issue of our role today as facilitators or road-blocks, as
help or hindrance, in a struggling church, is too widespread to ignore. There is too much at stake. And there is a
momentum in society and in our world today which is
ready to encourage us on a similar journey as themselves,
towards honest self-appraisal and to inspire us into a new
beginning.

To whatever extent we are guilty of falling down on the job
of effective and relevant ministry, of not rising to the challenges offered in the context of our belonging to an ailing
institution, or even of being regarded as (inadvertently)
working against progress, there is no malice in our hearts.
And rarely is there deliberate negativity, filibustering or
bad-mindedness in our reactions. Rather is there a great
deal of fear and ignorance of the unknown. That is why we
need to be re-educated, re-trained and re-skilled for being

church in a new kind of world. We see all around us just now, exciting and dynamic examples of appraisal, adjustment and creative strategies in the fields of business, education, communication, travel, sport and leisure. We need help to bring these enabling qualities and graces to our own situation. We need help at a whole number of levels. We need help especially in the skills of facilitating collaborative ministry in our parishes. This skill provides huge rewards. For the future of the church it promises a rich harvest. Without it, it will be a long and disastrous winter for us all, as we keep circling around in a hard-trodden space, using yesterday's implements for today's work, and generally misunderstanding the incarnational precariousness of our frail and flawed church, needing to be ever-renewed and re-routed if it is to find its place amid the traffic of a rushing world.

It is imperative that priests be drawn into new ways of thinking about the present threat to the church; that positive attitudes in the face of current crises and opportunities be encouraged and worked at; that every priest be offered the chance of equipping himself (together with his parishioners) with the tools for reading accurately the local and global signs of the times and, in the light of that reading, for putting new strategies in place. Each bishop, for example, has to convince his priests of the urgency of this need for new approaches and to provide suitable and professional courses to meet these needs. Only then will our insecurity begin to lessen its hold on us; only then will our frustration be partially eased; only then will we find the courage to face up to whatever must be addressed, because such knowledge, training and continuing support are very empowering, and bring with them a great sense of freedom and renewed confidence.

Faces of fidelity

This is a time for immense compassion for all priests who

are struggling with the current focus of their commitment and fidelity. Joan Chittister points out that of all the questions facing us today, the most important and troublesome is the question of fidelity itself. In a culture where change is swift and common, in a world where movement is global and given, in a society where three careers and two marriages are commonplace, the very notion of fidelity stretches us to the outside edge of meaning. The focus of our fidelity as priests, if it is to remain true to its original vision, must be revisioned and renewed in the light of a rapidly evolving world.

> The soul only grows as a result of the changes that tax and test our tolerance for the present. Change of mind, change of heart, change of hopes, change of insights require us, over and over again, to sort through all the pseudo-certainties of our life, keeping some things, altering others, discarding the rest of the notions that were once its convictions, its absolutes, the very staples of our souls. What once we thought fidelity was all about needs to be closely examined today ... Those who set about to stop the pace around them in the name of fidelity to the past have nothing to offer a world which the 'good old days' have passed by. The question is not to what were we asked to be faithful in the past. The question is to what must we be faithful in the present.[5]

Certainly, too much change runs the risk of destabilising the very ideas that undergird our lives and make change possible at all. Then there is nothing to steer by, nothing to count on, nothing to be sure of, nothing to maintain. Turmoil sets in with a vengeance. It happened, to a certain extent, when the Vatican II reforms, liturgical and theological especially, were introduced to an unprepared People of God. We are still suffering from this fact of church history. And many could not live with the sudden change. What happens at such threshold moments is that 'anomie' or 'acedia', the sense of a loss of purpose in life, of a 'giving up' on trying, begins to corrode the soul. Nothing matters much anymore. Anything goes. The feeling that anything is possible turns into the feeling that nothing is possible. Nevertheless, change depends on the certain understanding that there is a changeless foundation.

> Fidelity does not lie in refusing to change. Fidelity lies in making whatever changes are necessary to bring us from the ideals out of which we have always operated in order to achieve those ideals toward which we have always striven ... If a congregation itself warps the notion of fidelity by maintaining what is for its own sake, rather than making possible what must be for the sake of the gospel now, it is the congregation that has ceased to be faithful, not the members who prod it to fulfilment. 'If the church itself should become an obstacle to our salvation,' Thomas Aquinas writes, 'we would be required to leave the church.' Fidelity is not stability of place or function; it is stability of heart. It means being willing to change in order to remain the same.[6]

Just as, for instance, to be baptised or to be married is not just the living out of that one contractual moment in time, as an automatic 'given' for the rest of life, but implies a daily commitment to be true to the implications of that first covenant, so too with priesthood. The seminary training, the ordination ceremony, the first infusion of the 'character' of priesthood, are not like the winding up of a holy clock that will tick away, unerringly, for the rest of our lives, providing us with all we ever need to know in the face of rapid change at all levels. The grace and gift of ordination lies in the fact that it promises unfailing guidance, discernment and wisdom in the adaptations and adjustments we are daily called to make, in the unfolding evolution of human aspirations, technological progress, and universal becoming. Fidelity to the priesthood is about staying aware of what is going on in ourselves, around us, and in the world itself. It is about questioning, like the prophet does, the true value of everything along the way. It is about reading, as best we can, the signs of the times.

And often we fail. And often only failure can teach us what we really need to know about life. Is this not true for most of us in our experiences of being a priest? Being faithful is about the continuing need to choose between things, between things that are good as well as being bad, that are old as well as being new, so that we can commit ourselves always and anew, to the reign of God now, in ourselves and in the world, rather than simply to the adequate, the status quo, the merely sufficient to see us through another difficult patch.

> There is a difference between fidelity and endurance or tenacity. When we stay with something that is not good for us, simply to prove that we can endure what we no longer really love, what no longer really nourishes us to fullness of life, we do no favours to anyone, least of all to our own search for God and for the building up of God's reign in a very ambiguous and complicated world.

> Fidelity is not a style of life that suffers in silence for the sake of suffering. We are only truly faithful to what we are when we pursue the life of it with passion, sometimes with pain, but always with a willingness to pay the price, whatever the cost of coming to know our own smallness – as Moses did, as David did, as Jonah did – because life lived is worth the cost of it ... What we were born to be faithful to is no institution whatsoever, however exalted its claims. Fidelity, purely and simply, pursues from one stage, one place, one project to another, only the mind of

God and the passionate presence of the gospel, in a
world more comfortable with creeds rather than
with religion, more familiar with the church rather
than with the Christ, more committed to charity
rather than to justice, more enmeshed in oppression
rather than equality ...[7]

Tenacity and endurance, while worthwhile qualities at one
level, may well be found among the false faces of fidelity.
Sometimes, for instance, as priests, we have a hidden 'feel
good' factor about having 'stayed on' in our first commitment, when so many of our brother priests have 'left it'.
This is not what fidelity is about.

Fidelity isn't the fine art of gritting our teeth and
staying at something simply for the sake of staying
at it. Fidelity implies that we must work at being
what we say we will be, that we continue to give
ourselves to it even when it seems to be giving nothing back, provided that it is still worth the price of
our lives, provided that it remains a star to steer by,
provided that its end is the living God and not a
cheap facsimile ... The fruits of fidelity, of keeping
an eye on the heights, but being willing to slog
through soaked plains to get there, defy simple description. They dance and sing. They are freedom
from rigidity, they are freshness of thought, faith in
God, and fortitude under stress. Fidelity is the will-
ingness to perdure in crisis, to see a thing through, to
work it out, because working it out, making it work,
is something worth the grappling with.[8]

To be a priest today takes all the life we have left to live. To
be a priest today takes the heart of a hermit, the soul of a
mountain climber, the eyes of a lover, the hands of a healer,
the compassion of one who sees the whole world as a part
of himself. It requires total immersion in the life of Christ

and complete concentration on the meaning of the gospel values for a world gone astray. To be a priest today is to live out of a spirituality that colours his whole being.

> Spirituality is not the romantic rendering of a fanciful mysticism, an overdrawn religious imagination let loose upon the world to gush at it, or scold at it, or fuss at it. Spirituality is theology walking. Spirituality is what we do because of what we say we believe. What we dogmatise in creeds, spirituality enfleshes, and what we enflesh is what we really believe. If, for instance, we believe that the incarnation made all humanity holy, then we must be squarely on the side of those whose lives are undervalued, denigrated or derided. If we believe in the eucharistic community, then we must share the bread of our lives with those who are truly hungry and the wine of our days with those whose hearts lack the joys of life.[9]

Priesthood and imagination

A final word about the role of imagination, of creativity and of the mystical nature of the enterprise in hand. There are many reasons for spiritual writers to remind us of the 'toughness' of God's love and for the French novelist's description of priests as 'hard men'. And there are obvious reasons why rulers in general are at least uncomfortable with, if not fearful of, words and realities such as imagination, vision, beauty, creativity and those mystical properties that we metaphorically ascribe to the 'heart'. After all, the poet and the prophet are a menace on the assembly line! Nevertheless, maybe the Holy Spirit is gently reminding us of forgotten journeys we must be prepared to take; journeys into places and spaces within us that are longing to be found.

We are now in the land of the imagination. This land is so often tragically misunderstood. It is fundamental to our faith, and provides such a rich vein for the mining of our meditation. Who will write a book about the imagination of God, when playfully crafting the story and reality of creation and incarnation?

> A priesthood that is alive to the imagination finds itself in rhythm with the greatest sacrament of all, namely, the sacrament of life. It is the imagination that most truly holds to this rhythm. It brings the secret forms of our experience to visibility. Imagination allows the subtle divinity of our lives to unfold. This terrain between the visible and the invisible is where the priest works. Through the generosity and vulnerability of imaginative presence he helps people to behold the secret divinity of their lives, to sense the eternal light within, which no darkness can quench. This is very tender and patient work. There is no programme or special method which can elicit this vision. Only in the grace of real presence does it emerge, always shy and tentative, yet somehow always new and appropriate to the hunger that calls it forth ... Thus the great call in priesthood is the call homewards to this intimacy where there is neither shadow nor separation. This is the reason why priesthood is a graceful and gracious calling and is not to be confused with the repetitive, strained and mechanical externality of clericalism ... It is only through attention to the inner voice of experience that the priest can hear the whisper of God which the noise of modern culture drowns. This is the cause of the desperate spiritual hunger that rages today.[10]

For some years now, many of us have been painfully aware of the dislocation between the words we use in sermons and talks, and the reality of people's lives. Many decades ago Gregory Baum, a *peritus* at the Second Vatican

Council, reminded us of the need 'to cash our ecclesiastical language into the currency of lived experience'. And Karl Rahner, whose theology pervades the whole of this article, described our set homilies as 'dead birds falling from wintry skies'. How can all of us, baptised and ordained, bring the energy and vitality of the first Pentecost people to our community today? How can we recreate the Emmaus journey for all our companions on the road of life? But first, how do we come to believe in the divine spring waiting to be discovered in our own hearts?

Within the human sacred heart of Jesus the necessary cross gives birth to joy, the necessary darkness becomes the womb of light, and the necessary silence begins to sing. The promised abundant life is for here and for now. Without Christ, the spring as well as the water, without Christ, the human person as well as divine Son, without Christ, the sensitive lover as well as directive brother, without Christ, the imagination as well as the rule, all our priesthoods will one day die. Only by keeping the eyes of our hearts firmly fixed on our one role-model will the essence of our priesthood emerge. Only by immersing ourselves in the gospel accounts of the ministry of Jesus will we, too, find the balanced emphasis that will bring us true joy. And it is only by trusting the divine gifts of our imagination and creativity, as Jesus did in the face of the institutionalism and clericalism of his time, that we too will know for sure, by the peace in our hearts, that our energy is being channelled into healing and completing the most needy places in God's body today.

In his article about individuality and interiority, about each one's essential heart and soul, John O'Donoghue brings together the uses of imagination and the working of the Blessed Trinity. At its deepest level, he writes, individuality is shaped in the image of the Trinity which is the rhythm where the interflow of self and otherness enjoys its

highest intensity and possibility. The Trinity is the imagination that drew each shape and presence out of nothing-
ness. Everything and every person were formed and imag-
ined and sent here by the Trinity. Everything that is, is
within the Trinity; for there is nothing outside God. To
awaken this recognition requires a return to inwardness,
where in silence and solitude one's kinship with the invisible awakens. This has to be at the heart of evangelisation
in a fragmented, externalist western culture. This return to
the inner silence is not to be confused with introversion,
individualism or quietist navel-gazing. According to
O'Donoghue, there is a gentle irony in the fact that the
genuine return inwards is a coming home to where all belonging is rooted, where people and things, despite their
external separateness, are felt and known to be one – to belong together. The reign of God begins within. And its
evangelisation has to do with imagination.

> This theory of evangelisation would be loyal to
> imagination. The Holy Spirit is the Imagination of
> Life, the spirit who mediates between the frontiers of
> dark and light, between intimacy and otherness, be-
> tween fact and possibility, between being and noth-
> ingness, between death and eternity. Thus a doctrine
> of the Trinity is the most powerful affirmation of
> imagination. All imaginative activity, music, art, lit-
> erature, love and suffering are about the disclosure
> of the unexpected form in a matrix of experience and
> the ascetic process of allowing that to emerge. In
> fragmented culture, the artists are the secular priests
> and priestesses who keep the sacred alive, holding it
> in a form and a reserve from the vulgarity of modern
> immediacy.[11]

Faces of celibacy

Given the kind of sensitivity and intimacy within ourselves and with others that the above models of priest-

hood call for, it would be foolish and unrealistic to ignore the potential mine-field of debate regarding our celibate condition as priests. In the light of the often-prurient media interest in such matters, it is with great trepidation that any comments might be made. Oddly enough, maybe it is in the above reflection on the place of imagination and creativity in our lives as priests, that a word might be said about celibacy. Arising from the current plethora of discussions and books on the pros and cons of the celibate state, it seems fairly clear that there is much concern about 'the imposition of compulsory celibacy,' while the freely accepted charism of celibacy is universally regarded as a central chapter of witness in the eternal Christian story. Nevertheless, whatever the theological, ontological, philosophical and functional arguments regarding celibacy, there are many of us who, in our desire to become priests, took on, often quite unaware of the life-long significance, implications and never-ending struggle of such a commitment, the condition of celibacy. We are all well aware of the perennial reasons trotted out by various authorities on the subject for retaining forever this criterion for priesthood. However, in the light of what is happening amongst the brotherhood of priests today, and indeed in the findings of the *sensus fidelium* regarding mandatory celibacy, even in the most Catholic countries, there is little comfort for those who feel they have made a 'false sacrifice'.

But, without prejudicing the growing consensus among the people of God in this urgent debate and, perhaps more importantly just now, given the differing opinions of priests on this issue, and also without distinguishing too clearly between 'charismatic' celibacy (as knowingly requested and accepted) and mandatory celibacy (as imposed), what follows is offered as a kind of consoling reassurance for those of us who are in a state of ambiguity and confusion about the situation in which we find ourselves.

Maybe there is really no such thing as a false sacrifice – when it is made for God. To the divine eyes of compassion, no effort is unnoticed; nothing goes waste; all, in the end, is harvest. When 'the law is changed', as it probably will, (and as it already has, by implication) there is no need for any of us, no matter what our doubts or regrets may be, no matter how many times we have failed, no matter what the cost of the struggle to our personal fulfilment, to feel let down, misled or victimised. If every hair of our greying and balding heads is precious to God, and if every feather from a flying bird is lovingly noticed, so too, and infinitely more precious, is the act of blind trust and courage that set us out on this path in the first place, and that keeps us still trying to live up to that first commitment.

And even though not every priest is convinced of the value of his celibacy, there is a definite danger that, as we count the cost of it, in the real terms of perceived personality damage through suppression, sublimation, repression and denial, we may miss the blessing. We may miss the impact of the tough energy that is generated by celibacy in all kinds of ways – for our own spiritual maturity and that of others, for the hope that our witness affords to many hopeless people, broken and bitter from 'loves gone wrong', for a world seduced and betrayed by the urgent and demanding cult of individualism and by the relentless consumeristic drive toward instant gratification and fulfilment. If it is true that just one moment of a woman's silent sacrifice for her needy neighbour, or a man's last effort of endurance to provide for his family, reverberates forever around the halls of heaven, surely too our first act of faith (by embracing celibacy) in the reality of another lovely world, even more beautiful than this one, and our sometimes pathetic efforts to stay true to that original commitment, will carry a 'witness of glory' beyond our wildest dreams.

Therefore, flawed as the 'celibacy rule' may be and, for many of our brothers who claim to have been severely damaged by it, almost impossible to be fully lived out given the yearnings of our all-too-human hearts and bodies, what other public worldwide sign can testify to the values of another way of seeing things and of being fully human in a transcendent fashion, in the face of the unbelievable power of an often ruthless media, with its manipulating advertising and shallow mores, that leaves no one un- touched, including the churches themselves?

> (Celibacy) is not tied to any sense of ministry, effi- ciency, or 'victim offering', but appears to be a deep word of truth that is heard in the context of personal prayer and real sharing. It is a sense of vocation and integrity which, like all prophetic actions, has a hard time explaining itself or justifying itself to anyone else – and often even to the individual who has chosen it. It is an absolute newness, which says that God is sufficient, but it is also an absolute solitude, which says the world is lonely and passing away.[12]

Could it not be said that, beyond our individual failures and the current pressures to change the law of celibacy, something more eternal is at stake here? Is there not a danger of losing something very precious by a premature capitu- lation to a volatile, superficial and soul-less materialism? These reflections are not offered as an argument for retain- ing compulsory celibacy. They are offered as some kind of caution, in the light, for instance, of certain lost elements in the rushed reforms that happened after Vatican II (already mentioned) – a loss that many now regret and are trying to recover – liberating and life-giving that they all were, so as not to make the same mistake again. The question could be put in this way: if the Catholic Church, in her wisdom, over the past millennium set her store by the value of celibacy for all priests, with what will it be replaced?

In the meantime, to keep our hearts up, Joan Chittister offers this reflection. It is a liberating one because it links
celibacy with an autonomy and an inner authority that is
not always available to others. It has something to do with
seeing our role as beyond the strictures and the structures
of a competitive world, in a way that many others, in their
desperate struggle to survive, cannot always manage. We
are meant to be the 'free men' because we have nothing to
lose; we are meant to be 'in nobody's pocket' because nobody's pocket is big enough to contain God; we are the
ones who can always speak the truth without fear or
favour because it is not 'our own truth' we speak; we are
the ones who, no matter what the political or ecclesiastical
preferences of our congregations, can relentlessly, and at
the price of unpopularity or perceived failure, persevere in
promoting gospel values.

> The function of celibacy is not to be loveless; the
> function of celibacy is to love without limitation, to
> lay down my life in loving commitment to more
> than those who love me. The celibate can afford to be
> courageous. The celibate can afford to be rejected.
> The celibate can afford to be outside the systems and
> the servitude that hold others hostage to their re-
> sponsibility for the survival of others beyond them-
> selves … By opening us to love, wherever we find it,
> wherever it finds us, chastity puts the religious in
> the position of being the one person who bothers to
> see what others, with more focused eyes, may not.
> The passionate religious falls in love with soup
> kitchen people, and dirty kids, and grieving wid-
> ows, and dying AIDS patients, and dull and dour
> veterans of life, who have been loved so little that
> they themselves love not at all.[13]

What is important to note here is that the ordained priesthood holds no prerogative in such ministries. There is no

'playing down' of the role of the baptismal priesthood of all Christians. The only point being made is that if we look for a focus for such compassionate ministry, the role of the priest must surely be at the forefront.

The thrust of the preceding reflections presumes that celibacy is chosen, not imposed. That, of course, is the nub of the argument. But for those of us who claim to belong to the latter group, for those of us who feel sure that we were called to priesthood rather than celibacy as the first and fundamental option for the way we wanted to live our lives, maybe there is still some way in which we can, by a belated but sincere 'decision', by a kind of last-ditch effort, (and maybe all the more meaningful for that very reason) say a generous *fiat* now to what was all-unsuspectingly 'imposed' on us many years ago. Given the immediacy of God's free and unaccountable spirit of change and beginnings, is there not some way in which what was at the beginning 'not chosen', at a later time becomes 'chosen?'; some way in which what was originally 'mandatory' now becomes renewed as 'charismatic'; some way in which our yesterday-doubts and regrets can be transcended into a new tomorrow? Even for us, reluctant celibates, there is something irresistible about our witness.

> (As a charism) celibacy is the public face of contemplative experience making visible in this world the absolute freedom, the captivating beauty, the supreme generosity, and the ultimate fidelity of the divine love 'that moves the sun and other stars.' (Dante) Its life breath is prayer. Its ultimate explanation lies somewhere in the depths of Holy Mystery. And it is carried in fragile vessels of clay in order that it might be clear to all that the transcendent power is from God and not from us. (2 Cor 4:7)[14]

On a slightly lighter note, there are a few more observations to be made. We are told by those who are supposed to know about these things, that there is much 'elbow-room', so to speak, between absolute and total letter-of-the-law celibacy and full commitment to the permanently-loving and genital context of marriage. As celibates, we are not precluded from many kinds of intimacy with others. There is a sexuality that, whether we like it or not, pervades every encounter and relationship between men and women and, in some instances, between members of the same sex. This 'relationship space' is not to be interpreted as a 'license to fool around,' causing the kind of hurt and damage to others of which we are increasingly aware and may well be guilty, but as a recognition of the fact that to be truly human, as priests, we are free to relate deeply and personally to another, without making that person the sole reason for our security, our well-being, our fulfilment, our only focus for living. (Because relationship is a two-way heart-thing, there is no easy way, as many of us well know, to project a neat and clinical, unilateral and prescriptive outcome to such friendships, given our human condition and experiences.) James O'Keefe writes:

> Affective sexuality is the huge area of emotion, feelings and moods which move us towards another person – that which enables us to express tenderness, gentleness, warmth, compassion and openness to touch … Whatever it is we feel we need, celibacy is an invitation into vulnerability. We cannot say to anyone else, 'You are the ultimate person in my life. I will always be there for you alone,' and no one can say that to us. There is within everyone the yearning for unity, for oneness, for completeness – and we are not able to explore the fulfilment of this yearning with one person. So we are vulnerable, and most of us are not so good at being honest about this vulnerability. We can avoid the pain by living bachelor-hood-like lives – being single and unattached, but avoiding the real pain. We can hide behind status

and power, live lives of real physical comfort and variety, escape into substance-abuse of one kind or another – all rather than search out the path to genuine solitude and integrity.[15]

The reflections in James O'Keefe's article, like those in this book itself, arose from the honest sharing between priest friends. And there is no end to that sharing. Our only purpose in these pages is to reflect what is going on amongst us, in the present tense.

I am quite sure that, as a group, we were getting round to appreciating that we have to live celibacy in a conscious way, rather than let it lurk within us in an unconscious way. If we become more self-aware, and appreciate that celibacy is not simply about sexual activity, but more a whole way of life, then we can at least identify where our real needs are, rather than acting out something we do not fully understand. We saw it as tragic that we have been expected to live a celibate life more as an administrative decision than a journey in faith … Whatever else can be said about celibacy, it is certainly not an inherited condition and, as one priest said to his bishop after buying a three-quarter size bed, 'Well, I'm half expecting a change.'[16]

Jesus the Priest

It is high time to finish. All the above models, we hope, are true to the priesthood of Jesus, if only by way of hints half-understood. They are sketched against the canvas of his ministry, if only glimpsed through a glass darkly. Our role, in the end, is to promote his life's work, to preach what he preached, to reveal what he revealed, to be what he was, a man for others. Jesus did not stop at himself – he pointed beyond himself to his source, his centre, his horizon, his saving God. He was the sacrament of the omni-presence of

God in all creatures and in all things. The kind of evangelising he lived was to awaken people to the God at home in
their hearts already, and always, everywhere – a truth that
the 'penny catechism' starts off with. (Question 3)

Evangelisation is not about bringing God to a Godless
people. Albert Nolan refers to the footprints of God in
places long before the missionaries arrived there. The
good news is about the revelation to others of their own
divine hearts, of awakening people to the presence of God
in their midst, of bringing the already-indwelling Blessed
Trinity to their conscious awareness. To engage too soon in
the business of setting up churches and organised religion,
can prejudice the very essence of the gospel adventure.
However well-meaning our projects and efforts to increase
our numbers and reclaim our lapsed members, young and
old, unless the first gathering-place is in the domain of the
heart, there will be no lasting home-coming for those of us
who feel let down, alienated and disillusioned.

Jesus never made himself out to be an end in himself –
only in the sense that for Christians he is the one window
on to God, the face and heart and soul of his divine Parent,
the way home to heaven. His ministry sprang from his
self-awareness of the source of his being – and that self-
awareness was moulded in the cauldron of his many
inner, little deaths before the last one, his many little
break-throughs and transfigurations before his final one.
Like him, we too must travel through our inner and outer
barren deserts and the green fields of our lives' experiences. It is on the balance between these two inseparable
dimensions of the life of Jesus, and of ours, that these models
are hung. Our sure focus for maintaining this true balance
can only be the sacred, human heart of Our Lord and
Saviour, the vulnerable, invincible, anguished and ecstatic
ministry of Jesus, the priest.

With these thoughts in mind and with these reflections in

heart, we draw once again on the insights of John O'Donoghue. He reminds us that Jesus had a wonderful depth of sensitivity and imagination. All his language was fresh and alert. It was a language full of thresholds: it opened the heart to the eternal. His priesthood awakened the territories of imagination and divinity where the kingdom of love could grow.

As priest Jesus engaged without reserve the duality and ambivalence of our finitude. Time and again his presence evoked conflict and contradiction. Yet he never abandoned the precarious frontier where all dualities meet. He inhabited the nerve line of paradox and contradiction. We forget that Jesus knows contradiction, paradox and pathos from within. Despite the tension of the frontier he inhabited, he always kept his dignity, balance and poise. This must have been the fruit of the thirty years of solitary interior work before he emerged in his public mission...

His cross became the crucible which gathered the full intensity and outreach of human duality, negativity and contradiction. He wisely identified death as the wound in the universe, the wound from which all fear, diminishment and negativity flows. In embracing its full threat and destruction, he altered forever the grip of the negative on us. He transfigured it into a light-carrier and healer. The frontier becomes the place of greatest possibility and renewal. This is exactly the life force of transfiguration and healing that meets us in the sacraments. The sacraments are new thresholds where loss is transfigured into presence, darkness into light, fact to possibility and gravity to grace ...

One of the great challenges of priesthood is to hold to the implicit divinity of humanity. As a priest, Jesus witnessed to the inner priestliness of the individual which externality can neither name nor claim. He confronted and deconstructed the clericalism of contemporary Judaism. Time and again he unmasked its falsity and exposed the feeble perception behind its arrogance...

As a priest Jesus coaxed people back home to the hearth of their own interiority. He helped them in out of the exile of the external and awakened a new consciousness in them. He awakened their longing for the eternal but, unlike any previous preacher, he did not send them on a Sisyphian journey in search of a distant and unreachable divinity. Instead he showed us that we all live in the neighbourhood of the eternal. Everything we need for our journey is within the divine treasury of our interiority. Now there is an invitation and hunger for a priesthood of the heart...

Inspiration, wisdom and guidance are to be rediscovered in the priesthood of Jesus. He navigated beautifully the inner and outer thresholds. He dismantled clericalism, awakened the divine imagination, befriended and transfigured negativity and revealed the human body as the temple of the Holy Spirit.[17]

Comfortable and well-worn are my daily paths
whose edges have grown grey
with constant use.

My daily speech is a collection of old words
worn down at the heels
by repeated use.

My language and deeds, addicted to habit,
prefer the taste of old wine,
the feel of weathered skin.

Come, O you who are ever-new,
wrap my heart in a new wine-skin,
ever flexible to be reformed by your Spirit.

Set my feet to fresh paths this day;
inspire me to speak original and life-giving words
and to creatively give shape to the new.

Come and teach me to dance with delight
whenever your send a new melody my way.[18]

Some Discussion Points

1. What are your reactions to the section on clericalism and institutionalism? Why do many priests see it as an attack on the very meaning of their lives? If you agree with the critique, at what level can the situation be addressed?

2. The section on fidelity and commitment calls for a deep-seated change, a 'paradigm shift,' in our self-understanding as priests. Is this over-stated, or misplaced? Given the need for some kind of change in our approach to ministry, and using the graces of imagination and creativity, how would you describe the necessary development within our role as priest?

3. In light of the current debate about celibacy, this section was very difficult to write. Do you think it is a fair (if very limited) representation of how priests regard celibacy? What important aspects are badly dealt with, or completely omitted? What would you like to see included?

Notes

INTRODUCTION

1. Rather than provide an endless list of titles, I refer the reader to the following selection: *The Way Supplement*, 'The future of Ordained Ministry' 1995/83, available from Heythrop College, London; Thomas Lane, *A Priesthood in Tune*, The Columba Press 1993; James A. Fischer, *Priests: Images, Ideals and Changing Roles*, Dodd, Mead and Co. 1987; James H. Murphy (ed.), *New Beginnings in Ministry*, The Columba Press 1992; Donald Goergen (ed.), *Being a Priest Today*, Liturgical Press 1992; Donald Cozzens (ed.), *The Spirituality of the Diocesan Priest*, Liturgical Press 1997; William Bausch, *The Parish of the Next Millennium*, XXIIIrd Publications 1997; Andrew Irvine, *Between Two Worlds: Understanding and Managing Clergy Stress*, Mowbray 1997.
2. Lane p. 224.

PART I

1. Chittister, Joan, *The Flame in These Ashes*, Gracewing 1995, pp. viii,x.
2. ibid., pp. 54, 55.
3. O'Donoghue, John, 'To Awaken the Divinity Within: Towards a New Theory of Evangelisation', *The Way* Vol 34, Oct 1994, p. 266.
4. ibid., pp. 73, 76, 77.
5. Ryan, Seamus, 'Becoming More of Man…' *The Furrow*, Apr 1996.
6. Hoban, Brendan, 'Elephants in the Livingroom', *The Furrow*, Dec 1996.
7. Chittister, pp. 58, 59.
8. ibid., p. 64.
9. Hypher, Paul, 'Future Models of Ordained Ministry', *The Way Supplement* 1995. For a useful summary of the current debate about 'the two priesthoods', see Avery Dulles, *The Priestly Office*, chap. 1. See also *Lumen Gentium*, 10, 30-38, and the *Decree on the Apostolate of the Laity*.
10. Richards, Michael, 'Christian Priesthood', *The Tablet* Dec 17th 1990. (See also his *A People of Priests*, DLT 1995).
11. Lyons, Enda, *Partnership in Parish*, The Columba Press 1987.
12. See also Karl Rahner, *Theological Investigations*, vol 19, p. 80; vol 14, p. 208; Edward Schillebeeckx *Ministry*, pp.139-40, *The Church with a Human Face*, pp.119, 255-7, (quoted in Lyons, pp. 80-81); Raymond Brown *Priest and Bishop: BiblicalReflections*, Chapman 1971; Kenan Osborne *Priesthood: A History of Ordained Ministry in the Roman Catholic Church*, Paulist Press 1988.
13. Kelly, Tony, *An Expanding Theology*, E. J.Dwyer 1993; Enda McDonagh, *The Gracing of Society*, Gill and Macmillan 1989; Sally McFague, *Models of God*, SCM Press 1987.
14. Basil Hume, Address to Secondary Heads' Association, Cardiff Mar 1993.
15. O'Donoghue, p. 266
16. Gabriel Daly, *Creation and Redemption*, Gill and Macmillan 1988; James Mackey, *Modern Theology: A Sense of Direction*, OUP 1987;

Dermot Lane, *Christ at the Centre*, Veritas 1990; Michael Skelley, *The Liturgy of the World: Karl Rahner's Theology of Worship*, The Liturgical Press 1991; John Haught, *Mystery and Promise: A Theology of Revelation*, The Liturgical Press, 1993; Willigis Jager, *Search for the Meaning of Life – Reflections on the Mystical Experience*, Triumph Books 1995.

17. Regan, Frank, *Mission Spirituality in Vocation for Justice*, Spring 1997 (available from the Columban Mission.)

18. Macquarrie, John, *The Humility of God*, Westminister Press 1978; David Tracy, *Blessed Rage for Order*, Cambridge University Press 1970; Rene Latourelle, *Theology of Revelation*, Mercier Press Ltd., 1968. Enda Lyons, *Jesus: Self-portrait by God*, The Columba Press 1994.

19. Haught, John, *Mystery and Promise: A Theology of Revelation*, The Liturgical Press, p. 161

20. Berry, Thomas, *The Dream of the Earth*, Sierra Book Clubs 1988. Fritjof Capra and David Steindl-Rast with Thomas Matus, *Belonging to the Universe: Explorations on the Frontiers of Science and Spirituality*, Harper, San Francisco 1991; Bede Griffiths, *A New Vision of Reality: Western Science, Eastern Mysticism and Christian Faith*, Fount Books 1992; Rupert Sheldrake and Matthew Fox, *Natural Grace*, Bloomsbury 1996; Brian Swimme, *The Hidden Heart of the Cosmos*, Orbis1996.

PART II

1. O'Donoghue, 'The Priestliness of the Human Heart', *The Way Supplement*, 1995.

2. Grufferty, Tom, Letter to *The Tablet*, 17 May 1997.

3. O'Donoghue, ibid., p. 44.

4. Barron, Robert, 'The Priest as Bearer of Mystery', *The Furrow*, Apr 1995.

5. For further relevant reading see K. Lehmann and A Rafflet (eds)., *Karl Rahner; The Practice of the Faith*, SCM Press, 1985.

6. Lane, p. 301.

7. Harries, Richard, *Art and the Beauty of God*, Mowbray 1993, p. 87.

8. ibid., p. 62.

9. Hughes, Gerard, *Oh God Why?*, The Bible Reading Fellowship 1993.

10. Tessimond, A. S., 'The Deaf Animal' from Selection Putnam 1958: quoted in *Children in Search of Meaning*, Violet Madge, SCM Press 1965, p. 102.

11. O'Donoghue, ibid., p. 46.

12. Sellner, Edward, *Mentoring: The Ministry of Spiritual Kinship*, Ave Maria Press, 1990 p. 61. Also see the recent works of Robert Bly, Richard Rohr, Sam Keen and Joseph Campbell on this subject.

13. For an introduction to such evidence see Kenneth Leech *Soul Friend: The Practice of Christian Spirituality*, Harper and Row 1980; Aelred of Rivaulx, *On Spiritual Friendship*, Consortium Press 1974; Thomas Merton, *New Seeds of Contemplation*, New Directions 1961; Alan Jones, *Soul-Making*, Harper and Row 1985; Rainer Maria Rilke *Letters to a Young Poet*, W.W. Norton Press 1934.

14. Rohr, Richard, *Near Occasions of Grace*, Orbis Books 1993, p. 54.
15. Vanier, Jean, *Community and Growth*, DLT 1980, pp. 171, 179.
16. Edwards, Tilden, *Spiritual Friend*, Paulist Press 1980, pp. 145, 128.
17. Zipfel, Paul, 'Priesthood, Listening and the Music', *Review for Religious*, Oct 1992.
18. Ó Ríordáin, John J., *The Music of What Happens*, The Columba Press, 1996, p. 7.
19. Vanier, p. 248.
20. McDonagh, Sean, 'God's Planet Too', *The Catholic Herald* 13 June 1997. See his *To Care for the Earth*, Chapman 1986, and *The Greening of the Church*, Chapman 1990. Also Philip Joranson and Ken Butigan (eds), *Cry of the Environment: Rebuilding the Christian*, Bear and Co. 1984.
21. Boucher, Peter, 'Preaching Jesus Christ Today', *The Furrow*, May 1997.
22. Rohr, pp. 108, 109.
23. ibid., p.109.
24. West, Morris, *The Clowns of God*, Coronet Books 1981, p. 425.
25. Rohr, p. 109.
26. Vanier, p. 44.
27. Rohr, p. 110.
28. Vanier, p. 192.
29. Nolan, Albert, *Jesus Before Christianity*, Orbis Books 1978, p.125.
30. From Donal Lucey's letter to the eds.

PART III
1. Kilcoyne, Colm, Article in *The Sunday Tribune* 8 Oct 1995.
2. O'Donoghue, ibid., p. 47.
3. Hypher, op. cit.
4. Dubay, John J., 'Clericalism', *The Furrow* Jun 1997 (see also Ann Wilson Schaef, *The Addictive Organisation*, Harper and Row 1988).
5. Chittister, pp. 78, 79.
6. ibid., pp. 80, 81.
7. ibid., pp. 85, 86.
8. ibid., pp. 87, 88.
9. ibid., p.103.
10. O'Donoghue, op. cit., p. 49.
11. O'Donoghue, To Awaken..., p. 269.
12. Rohr p. 42. For an introduction to the detailed examination of the current debate about charismatic and mandatory celibacy, etc., see the1993 issue of *The Way Supplement* 81, 'Celibacy'.
13. Chittister, pp. 23, 120.
14. Schneiders, Sandra, 'Celibacy as Charism', *The Way Supplement* 93, p. 24.
15. O'Keefe, James, Living with Compulsory Celibacy, *The Way Supplement* 1993 p. 40.
16. ibid., pp. 44, 45.
17. O'Donoghue, The Priestliness..., pp. 51, 52.
18. Hayes, Edward, *Prayers for a Planetary Pilgrim*, Forest of Peace Books Inc., 1989, p.147.